MAXIMUM MARRIAGE

28 Couples Share
Their Secrets for a Happy Marriage

Peggy and Roger Dudley

REVIEW AND HERALD® PUBLISHING ASSOCIATION
HAGERSTOWN, MD 21740

The authors assume full responsibility for the accuracy of all facts and quotations as cited in this book.

Texts credited to Clear Word are from *The Clear Word,* copyright © 1994 by Jack J. Blanco.

Texts credited to NIV are from the *Holy Bible, New International Version.* Copyright © 1973, 1978, 1984, International Bible Society. Used by permission of Zondervan Bible Publishers.

Bible texts credited to NRSV are from the New Revised Standard Version of the Bible, copyright © 1989 by the Division of Christian Education of the National Council of the Churches of Christ in the U.S.A. Used by permission.

This book was
Edited by Jeannette R. Johnson
Designed by Tina Ivany
Cover designed by Square One Design
Cover photo by Joel D. Springer
Typeset: 11/14 Berkeley Old Style

PRINTED IN U.S.A.

07 06 05 04 03   5 4 3 2 1

R&H Cataloging Service
Dudley, Roger, 1931-
     Maximum marriage: 28 couples share their secrets for a happy marriage,
By Roger and Peggy Dudley.

     1. Marriage.   2. Married people.   I. Dudley, Peggy, 1931-   .   II. Title.

                    306.81

ISBN 0-8280-1758-1

❖   ❖   ❖

Also by Roger Dudley:

Why Our Teenagers Leave the Church

To order, call 1-800-765-6955.

Visit us at www.reviewandherald.com for information on other Review and Herald® products.

THIS BOOK IS LOVINGLY DEDICATED TO

John and Millie Youngberg

Their inspirational ministry has blessed not only our lives and home but that of thousands of others. They will humbly say, "There has been no 'merit' in our work. All the glory belongs to God. If there was any virtue, it was tenacity."

John and Millie were pioneers in marriage commitment seminars, marriage commitment seminars leadership, family life workshops, Operation Family, Transmitting Religious Heritage, Family Wellness, Child Rearing and Discipline seminars. (Does this lengthy list amaze you as it does us?)

During the past 28 years they've conducted 160 Marriage Commitment seminars, with 2,700 couples attending. They've trained 1,500 leaders so that they, in turn, can continue this wonderful work of marriage building in their own milieus. They've published more than 20 books in nine languages on family life and produced a 14-video series entitled *Enriching Family Devotions*. Their motto, "We Gladly Share," is evident in the materials they've prepared that are audience-ready and in a seminar format.

They've been an inspiration to us as we've watched their tireless efforts to strengthen the family. It's been our privilege to take their leadership course, to co-conduct several seminars with them, and then to hold many more on our own.

> "But before that great and terrible day of the Lord comes,
> I will send a message such as I gave to Elijah,
>   calling the people to choose whom they will serve.
> This message will be taken to the whole world.
>   It will knit my people together,
>   and the hearts of the fathers will turn in love to their children,
>   and the hearts of the children will turn in love to their fathers.
> And though the earth is set aside for destruction, my people will be saved."
>   —Malachi 4:5, 6, *Clear Word*

CONTENTS

WHY THIS BOOK?

The sad-looking couple came into my counseling office. Their marriage was in deep trouble, and they were talking divorce. It wasn't a question of an affair with a third party; they just weren't getting along. I asked for examples. They raised several points that I considered minor. The one I remember best was the struggle over the placement of the stereo in the living room. He would put it in one place; she would move it to another. He would move it back. She would replace it. And so it went. Very petty, but it was really symbolic of a power struggle.

Finally I asked him how committed he was to the marriage. "Roger, I don't care about it at all," he replied. "I want out. I came here only because a friend said I should see a counselor before I divorce."

Not being a miracle worker, I couldn't save that union. Unfortunately, this couple is representative of many. The little annoyances that marred this relationship seem so insignificant when viewed in the larger perspective of a lifelong relationship. But when you are hurting, it's hard to take the long-term view.

Everyone wants to be happy, and most people believe that marriage is the road to get there. A couple is *so* in love, delighted that they have finally found Mr. or Ms. Right. All their worries are over, and they contemplate a life of never-ending bliss.

Then the honeymoon ends, and they begin to discover that life isn't a bowl of cherries, after all. Life presents challenges. The couple faces the difficulties of struggling with finances; balancing work and family; rearing children; dealing with in-laws; and meeting each other's social, emotional, and sexual needs.

Back in 1980 the Review and Herald published our book *Married and Glad of It*. In it we described how we became involved in Adventist Marriage Enrichment and how that experience changed our relationship. We tried to share what we had learned. In the years since then much has happened to us as a couple and to our culture. We have conducted numerous marriage seminars, held workshops, and counseled with many individuals and couples. A realization that emerged was how often couples enter into marriage without realizing how much work is involved in adjusting to each other's differences.

Those who have done premarriage counseling may have discovered, as we have, that many couples think that what really matters is that they are in love. After marriage their expectation is that they will simply do what comes naturally and live happily ever after. Then, inevitably, the DREAM stage of marriage passes and, with the advent of reality, DISILLUSIONMENT often sets in. At this juncture many decide that the problem is that they have married the wrong person.

Their solution is often to divorce and find someone else who is easier to get along with. While it is difficult to determine the divorce rate in America precisely, the percentage of divorces to marriages has risen dramatically from the levels of the mid-twentieth century. Adventists are not immune either. Several large studies in which Adventist young people have been asked about the marital status of their parents indicate a divorce rate of about 25 percent. In some cases the couple doesn't divorce but withdraws psychologically from each other to live separate lives—a condition that has been called "married singles."

Our solution was to write this sequel to the 1980 book. Rather than write about the problems couples face, we wanted to share positive examples from real life that demonstrate problem-solving skills. We wanted to write a book about successful, actual life experiences that would illustrate that good marriages don't just happen—they represent hard work. But the effort is so very worthwhile. We wanted these stories to be written by couples who are happily married. So we interviewed couples who had faced problems and concerns, just as any ordinary people do, but who didn't throw in the towel. They not only survived; they flourished.

We are excited about the stories these couples have shared with us, and want to share them with you. We appreciate their willingness, more than we can tell, to make themselves vulnerable in the hope of helping others. Their motivation is to encourage couples to stay married, to work through their challenges instead of giving up. And that is our motivation as well, to help couples move from DISILLUSIONMENT to the DISCOVERY of the positive traits of their mates. To take the focus off their faults and put it onto their strengths. The result will be a marriage where love gains DEPTH with each passing year. This is our prayer for each one of our readers.

For a full discussion of the DREAM, DISILLUSIONMENT, DISCOV-
ERY, and DEPTH sequence, see David Augsburger, *Sustaining Love:
Healing and Growth in the Passages of Marriage* (Ventura, Calif.: Regal
Books, 1988), pp. 70-96.

Chapter 1

SETTING PRIORITIES

Peggy and Roger's Story

When Laura and Mark were dating, they couldn't get enough of each other. Every spare minute during the day they were with each other. Then in the evenings they spent hours talking on the phone. When they had to be separated, they wrote every day.

Then they married. At first they continued to spend big chunks of time with each other. But as the months rolled by, other things demanded their attention. They both secured jobs that kept them busy most of the day. Evenings were taken up with housework, bills, newspapers, and television. They began to invest time in other friendships. Then the children began arriving and demanded much of Laura's energy and the little leisure that remained.

As the years progressed Laura and Mark found their lives becoming more and more separate. While the marriage was not threatened, they had lost the closeness of courtship. The magic, the romance, the intimacy, and even the companionship that they once enjoyed was essentially gone.

If a marriage is to be successful and fulfilling, both partners need to set priorities and live by those priorities. Is your marriage more important than anything else, except God? Is it more important than your job? than the extra luxuries money can buy? than getting an advanced degree? than your hobbies? than your other friendships? than your children?

These are hard questions that require some earnest soul-searching. No hasty, flippant answers will do. If push came to shove, would you *really* rather have a loving, happy marriage—or a fabulous career? Would you prefer to spend leisure time with your male or female friends, or would you rather plan your recreation with your spouse? Are you likely to put all your energies into your children, or is it a higher priority to nurture the marriage that provides their security and model for their adult lifestyle? Would you rather get good grades at school, or have a heavenly marriage?

If, after careful consideration, you arrive at the conviction that you would lose almost anything else before you would let your marriage go, then you will have to do something about it. No relationship can thrive and grow without spending both quality and quantity time together. You will have to deliberately and intentionally carve out time to be together, to engage in those activities that enhance relationships. Someone has said that "love is a four-letter word spelled t-i-m-e."

This is not going to be easy—especially for those with open-ended jobs where they do not punch in and out at stated times. The demands of a career, getting ahead, satisfying the boss and the customers/clients/parishioners, etc., can easily sap time away from the marriage. These are urgent and must be dealt with while the marriage is still intact and can be nurtured another day. The married student must spend time studying in order to prepare for that dream job. It's for only a few years, and then time can be devoted to the marriage. You have to take time with the children; they have so many needs and in a few years they will be gone. Then, as empty nesters, the husband and wife will have time for each other.

If you do decide that your marriage comes first, after God, that you will fight the fierce current of intrusions, then find a way to live by the priorities you believe in and do not be pulled aside by every distraction—no matter how urgent or pressing. Let us tell you part of our story.

Roger: As a young college student studying for the ministry, I was strongly impressed with the sacredness and importance of God's calling. My teachers related stories of sacrifice and devotion in mission and urged us to give of ourselves unselfishly for the finishing of God's work. Nothing could equal in importance the salvation of lost men and women. I emerged from college with high ideals and a lofty concept of ministry. Somehow, though, I failed to balance this zeal with the importance of family. I failed to temper my vocational zeal with what deep down was vital to me—my wife and daughter. For a number of years (I'm ashamed to tell you how many) I operated on the principle that "the work" must always come first.

I loved Peggy very much, but I expected her to understand that as a minister's wife she must make sacrifices. What's more, she should make them willingly and cheerfully. Wasn't that what our life calling was all about? Sometimes I would be gone days at a time. I would be out most evenings. When I was home I would have to be studying or doing other "crucial" tasks that didn't involve the family. I knew nothing about "taking a day off." Sabbath was always a heavy day, often with several speaking appointments. "Family time" meant dragging my wife and daughter along to hear me speak several times. And even on Sundays I studied, visited Pathfinder clubs, or attended important conference events.

Peggy felt terribly lonely and neglected. Worse yet, she suffered guilt feelings for feeling that way. Wasn't she supposed to be happy to make sacrifices for "the Lord's work"? Maybe her loneliness and unhappiness meant that she wasn't really consecrated. I'm afraid that I did little to reassure her. I didn't know any other way to operate.

Then came the awakening. As a conference director of youth ministries, I was working with a group of teenagers and young adults in a series of Voice of Youth meetings. The meetings were being held in a large tent about 150 miles from our home. One morning I received an urgent phone call. Peggy was calling from the hospital. She had developed a problem that would require surgery. While the condition was not serious, she would have to undergo general anesthesia. She was frightened and alone.

But we had a crucial meeting scheduled for that evening. "If you need me, I'll come now and skip the meeting," I offered.

In her fear and uncertainty she needed me, all right—desperately. But good Christian girl that she was, she knew the appropriate answer. "No, I'll be OK. You stay for the meeting; I know it's important. But please pray for me."

Of course she was hoping against hope that I would say, "No, you are more important," and that I would jump into my car and race to her side as quickly as possible. That's what I should have done—but I didn't. My training and mind-set allowed me to accept the spoken message and ignore the heart cry that I was too insensitive to hear. I did drive home late that night and visited her in the hospital the next morning. Then it was back to the tent. She was in the hospital for several days, during which time I squeezed in another visit or two, always sandwiching them in between the "really important work."

It wasn't until later, with the meetings over and Peggy back from the hospital, that she found a way to tell me about how afraid and lonely she had been. I began to realize for the first time just how far I had drifted from an understanding of what really mattered most to me. I knew that I had to make some changes in my life. I decided that my wife would be my first priority after God, and that I needed to block out significant quality time for her and for our daughter. We began to schedule times to do things together, and to nourish our relationship.

I wish I could report that my "conversion" was permanent, and that I never lost sight of my priorities after that. However, human growth does not take place in a single bound. With new insights we tend to make gradual—and sometimes slow—progress, with slip-backs along the way. How wonderful that the good Lord is patient with us! I needed a few more experiences to bring me back to those priorities that would eventually come to mean the most.

As a conference youth ministries director I was in charge of our youth camping programs. Those who have worked at a summer camp know that it is a seven-days-a-week job. On Sunday the campers arrive. They are very excited and eager to savor the new experiences, and the staff members have to be continually on their toes in order to channel the boundless youthful energy into constructive activities. By the end of the week everyone is pretty well worn out. The tired campers check out on Sunday morning to go home and get some needed rest, but the staff gets no rest.

They face a new bunch of lively youngsters who arrive right on the heels of the departing ones.

As camp director I felt that I had to be in charge every minute. I needed to serve all seven days, from starting things off with morning reveille to the final taps and making sure everyone else went to sleep. I was indispensable. Of course, this meant complete neglect of wife and family. But I was sure that if I left camp, everything would fall apart.

Peggy took it as long as she could; then one day she had a little talk with me. She reminded me about our decision to give each other and our family priority and not to let work crowd out the time we needed together. So I decided to do a daring thing: I would take off one day a week. I would put another staff member in charge and come home, and we would spend the day together.

What a great time we had! We went to the city to view interesting places, did some projects together, dined out, and played games we both enjoyed. The amazing thing was that when I finally returned to camp, I found that everything was going smoothly. I don't think they even missed me. So much for being indispensable! Someone can always replace you in the work force, but nobody can ever replace you in the special marriage relationship you create by shared memories over time.

By now you'd think I would have learned my lesson. But old habits die hard. We moved to a new state where I was a teacher at a boarding academy. I was given a heavy load: Bible teacher, school counselor, religious activities sponsor, and Student Association cosponsor. Those first six weeks, while I was getting a handle on my new job, pretty well consumed me. Then one day as I dragged myself wearily into the house, Peggy said she would like to talk with me. She took me gently by the hand, led me to the couch, and sat me down. Her communication was simple, direct, and without any sense of blame: "I don't feel special anymore."

How those few words cut into my conscience! In a flash it came to me that I had abandoned all my past resolutions and turned my priorities upside down. We decided to start over. That Saturday night a special Student Association program was scheduled, one in which I would have sponsorship duties. However, I told my cosponsor that I could not be present. I simply had a prior commitment. Peggy and I took off Sabbath morning and headed for the mountains. We spent the whole day walking nature trails hand in hand, singing praise choruses, worshiping God, and enjoying the beauties of nature. We came back revived and refreshed and with a new determination to make each other first in our priorities.

A couple years later we attended our first Marriage Encounter seminar. Then we attended Adventist Marriage Enrichment, Marriage Commitment seminars, and several others. We became marriage seminar leaders and have conducted dozens of seminars, helping hundreds of couples. But the couple we helped most was ourselves, because we learned how to communicate inner feelings and to let each other know what we needed in the relationship.

Since then we have tried to give each other the highest priority, next to God, in our marriage. When I did my doctoral studies and worked as a graduate assistant, Peggy worked at a full-time job and typed my papers in the evenings. We had a very heavy schedule and were under considerable pressure. Yet we set aside an hour every evening to spend with each other. We would walk and pray together, and we tried to do fun things at least once a week. Today (though we sometimes fail) we try to put our relationship first. I am often invited to go on speaking or other business trips. I never take one that will keep me away more than a few days. On any invitations for overseas assignments I make it clear that unless Peggy goes, I don't go either.

My reformation has made it possible for us to come to 50 years of marriage as best friends. We eat together every day, sleep together every night, date nearly every week, work together on ministry projects, engage in recreation together, and *always* vacation together. Those jobs I once held are long gone, but I still have Peggy.

Peggy: Those early days were indeed lonely and long and exhausting. I tried to take care of our daughter's needs, our home, and our yard. It seemed that we just worked and worked all the time. I too thought that that was the way it was supposed to be when one was married to a minister. And, as Roger said, I thought there was something wrong with me because I was not feeling fulfilled or enjoying life. There was something truly missing—companionship, working together as a husband and wife, and making home a pleasant place for our daughter.

Where was the communication? The truth of the matter is I didn't know how to communicate without sounding critical. I didn't know about using "I" messages and just sharing feelings without blaming, so I just re treated into my silent self. The last thing I wanted to create was conflict— I had seen enough of that in my childhood. There had been no models in my growing-up years from whom to learn the right way. But praise the Lord, we learned those skills while attending marriage seminars and reading books about marriage. These did not become available until we were in midlife. Before that, rarely did anyone talk or write about such deeply private things as one's marriage.

We were attending Marriage Encounter and listening to a couple dialogue about their communication. The husband was explaining to his wife how he felt when she retreated into her silent self. His description really opened my eyes so that I could begin to understand how puzzling my behavior was to Roger.

He said to his wife, "Do you know what it feels like to be looking into a window when someone pulls the blinds down in front of your face? That's how I feel when you become silent, and I can't figure out what is going on."

Before this "aha" experience I would wonder why Roger couldn't figure out what was bothering me without my having to tell him. It seemed so obvious to me! Now I know that there is often a gender difference in the way events are interpreted. Many men reason things out from a logical stance, while women often reason things out from a relational point of view. And no one should be expected to read another's mind.

Once we learned these skills I was able to talk with Roger about our relationship in a way that was not an attack or blaming. And Roger learned to listen and accept my feelings without trying to convince me that they were illogical. I realized that I also had responsibility for the way we lived our lives. There were times I fell into the same trap of skewed priorities. Indeed, there were times Roger felt less important than my doctoral studies or work demands. But with improved communication skills it was not so difficult to make the adjustments when priorities became skewed. We learned that life is constantly changing, and so must our adjustments to these changes. I now truly feel that I am Roger's highest priority, next to God, and I work on letting Roger know that in the same way he is mine.

Chapter 2

HER NEEDS, HIS NEEDS

Karen and Dwight's Story

Why do people get married? What keeps them in the marriage relationship over the long years? Why do some couples give up on the marriage and look elsewhere?

Motivational psychologists say that human beings are goal-driven. All of us have been created by God with certain needs. These needs can be basic physical ones—safety, esteem, love and belonging, group affiliation, fulfillment of potential, etc. Some students of personal motivation, such as Abraham Maslow, have arranged these needs in a hierarchical order, depending on their primacy and intensity to satisfying living. All human behavior is an attempt to reach goals that will satisfy these needs. No one will continue in a course of action that is not perceived as meeting some fundamental need.

The Bible has much in common with psychology, because both deal with the deepest human longings, aspirations, and fears. This merger can be read at its best in Philippians 4:19: "And my God will fully satisfy every need of yours according to his riches in glory in Christ Jesus" (NRSV). That's a wonderful promise! Our needs are part of our creation–they are fully legitimate.

People often try to satisfy these needs in ways that are self-destructive (misbehaving in school, drug abuse, promiscuity, marital infidelity). God, on the other hand, has made provision to satisfy every need in ways that will promote physical, spiritual, emotional, and social health. While He has many ways of doing this, He often uses the agency of other people in our life space. This is obviously true in the parent-child relationship, but also in the union of husband and wife.

In the very first wedding sermon God said, "Therefore a man leaves his father and his mother and clings to his wife, and they become one flesh" (Genesis 2:24, NRSV).

THE SERMON

Dwight Nelson, senior pastor of the Pioneer Memorial church on the campus of Andrews University, preached a series of sermons on marriage and family. Toward the end of the series his wife, Karen, joined him in the pulpit to codeliver a message entitled "His Needs, Her Needs—Five Secrets to a Lasting Marriage."

The Nelsons were open and vulnerable about their own marriage. Both strong personalities with strong opinions, they have had to work through conflicts and difficulties. Dwight told how he had fallen in love with Karen in college and married her, expecting a life of bliss. But the first year was rocky. Studies show that the first year of married life has the highest incidence of divorce of any single year. At one point he sighed, "Now I understand why Jesus and Paul were single." In marriage you are supposed to become one. The trouble is which one?

The turning point came when he realized that he could not change Karen to fit his model; he could change only himself. What was needed was self-effacing love. The Genesis passage said the husband should cling to his wife. If a couple will cling to each other and to God, there is no mountain they can't climb.

The Nelsons found encouragement in a book by Willard F. Harley, Jr., *His Needs, Her Needs: Building an Affair-proof Marriage.* Harley explains that we all have a love bank. Mates make either deposits or withdrawals in each other's bank. In nearly every encounter they affect each other emotionally in ways that are either positive or negative. Husbands and wives need to study each other and become aware of their needs. They need to ask how they can best meet the legitimate needs of their spouses. By doing this, they build up massive accounts in the love bank and make their marriages affair-proof and divorce-proof. More than that, their married life becomes highly satisfying and fulfilling.

The Nelsons then presented the top five needs of both women and men, according to Harley. Couples who will work on supplying these needs can build a great marriage, regardless of personality differences or areas of disagreement. Their personal testimonies were heartwarming.

HER NEEDS

1. *The first need of a wife is affection.* Some men aren't very sentimental and see little need to constantly reassure their wives of their love. They are like the man who said, "When we got married, I told my wife that I loved her, and if I change my mind I'll let her know." Wives thrive on romance and need daily assurance that they are first in their husbands' affections. They need messages of love.

Karen sometimes finds such messages written on the bathroom mirror or taped to her pillow. Here are some suggestions they shared:

◆ At least 10 times a day, tell your wife that you love her. Tell her how wonderful she is and how lucky you are that she chose you (needs for esteem, love, and belonging).

◆ Wake up every morning with a hug and kiss. Always kiss and hug whenever you part and when you come back together. Hold hands when you walk together. Give her a hug or a friendly pat whenever you walk by her.

◆ Wink at her across the room.

◆ Do romantic things, such as inviting her to sit on your lap while you watch television or a video.

◆ Karen is in her glory when Dwight gives her a back rub.

We know that some of you are going to say that this is silly, mushy stuff. But that may be just what your marriage needs. Dwight and Karen report that these things really build up deposits in her love bank. A wife who has been romanced is ready to meet her husband's sexual needs. (More about that later.) Most women don't respond to sexual invitations when there has been no prior loving interaction. Someone has said that if you want a satisfying sexual experience in the evening, you need to start in the morning.

2. *A wife's second need is for conversation.* A wife wants her husband to talk to her. She is turned off with mere grunts. She needs her mate to listen to her. Men tend to hide their feelings and discuss logical things such as politics and sports. Most women are more expressive. They need to vent their feelings. Right here is where many men go wrong. When their wives share something, they want to suggest a solution, or fix the problem. Karen said that she has to tell Dwight, "I don't want you to fix it, or to tell me what to do. I just want you to listen to me. I need a sounding board. If I later want some advice, I'll ask you for it." Every time a man listens sympathetically to his wife and takes an interest in what she is sharing, he is putting deposits in her love bank.

3. *A wife's third need is for her husband to be honest and open.* She needs to know that he is dependable and predictable. She can count on him. The husband must not keep back anything that might concern her. She needs to know about his work, his plans, and the family finances. Wives don't want big surprises of an unpleasant nature. If there is a crisis situation, let him make full disclosure, and let them tackle it together.

This suggests *vulnerability*. Karen appreciates it when Dwight lets her into his deepest thoughts and aspirations. After God had delivered the concise wedding sermon in Genesis 2:24, the next text states, "And the man and his wife were both naked, and were not ashamed" (verse 25, NRSV). Many Bible interpreters have held that this applies not just to physical nakedness but to emotional and psychological openness and vulnerability. Dwight and Karen say that your mate should know you better than anyone else in the world.

4. *A wife needs to know that she has financial support.* Even in these days of gender equality, with more and more women entering the work force and earning their own money, she needs to know that her husband will provide for her. This is related to the basic psychological need for safety

and security. Will her husband manage their finances well? Will he not put them in economic straits by making unwise financial decisions or wasting their income on grown-up "toys"? Can she rest assured that the harmony of the home will not be disturbed by bill collectors hounding them? Dwight says that when it comes to marriage and money, less may be more. That means that both the husband and wife should lower demands for "stuff" in order that the family accounts will be "in the black."

5. *Finally, the wife needs family commitment from her husband.* This commitment is, first of all, to her as a person. She needs to know that the marriage is unbreakable. No matter what crises arise or problems develop, her husband will never entertain thoughts of leaving the marriage. She has the security of knowing that for him it is "until death do us part."

Second, that commitment is to the children. Though Dwight is a very busy pastor and world-renowned speaker, he recommends that the father spend at least 15 hours a week with children who are still in the home. This can include eating together, worship, church attendance, recreation, and plain, honest dialog. Wives feel secure when they know that their husbands take a real interest in family matters. Karen says that "the best husband is a good father."

His Needs

Quite a list! What a challenge for a husband who wants to meet his wife's legitimate needs. However, marriage is a two-way street. He also has needs, and in a happy, stable marriage she will try to supply them.

1. *The husband has a need for sexual fulfillment.* Harley puts this at the top of the list. God has created males with such a strong sexual drive that it is doubtful that a marriage can be affair-proof without this need being met. Dwight and Karen say that when it comes to sex (male's number one) and affection (female's number one), "you can't have one without the other." Marriage specialists have said that "women give sex to get affection, and men give affection to get sex." Thus, there is a mutual meeting of needs that results in the kind of intimacy that affair-proofs the marriage. We consider this topic important enough that we will devote another chapter in this book to the subject.

2. *The second need for the husband is recreational companionship.* Before marriage many couples spend hours together and do almost everything as

a team. After marriage there is a tendency for the two to gradually go their separate ways. He wants to hunt, fish, play golf, or go bowling. She likes gatherings with her female friends. As they grow older, they grow apart and become "married singles."

The Nelsons urge couples to find activities that they both enjoy. They personally like hiking, camping, and sailing. "Have fun together," they plead. With a new twist on an old maxim, they claim that "the couple that plays together stays together."

3. *The third male need is for an attractive spouse.* Of course, we all suffer the ravages of aging, and the wife at 50 cannot quite match her looks as the bride of 20. "But," Dwight says, "she should resemble the woman he married." She should not let herself get out of shape physically. She should continue to be mentally sharp and interesting, and she should wear clothes that bring out her best features. (Of course, this applies to men, too.) Overhanging bellies and loose flab do little to attract a couple to each other. Especially at bedtime, the Nelsons say, she should discard those baggy, fading flannels and dress attractively.

4. *The fourth male need is for domestic support.* If the husband works hard all day as the main provider, he doesn't want to come home to a messy house, refrigerator leftovers, and an evening of stress and arguments. The husband needs a home where the atmosphere is peaceful and stress-free, where the house is orderly, and where he can find the nutritious meals he needs to keep going in the world "out there."

The Nelsons recognize that in modern Western society more and more women are working outside the home, usually because of financial necessity. Karen has a full-time job as a nurse. In such cases the wife cannot be expected to come home after a full day in the labor market and tackle all the meal preparation, housecleaning, laundry, and child care. In two-working-spouses marriages, a couple must work out an arrangement in which all family responsibilities are somewhat equally shared. If the husband fills the role of primary provider, than the wife may be seen as chief executive and organizer of home duties. Dwight is especially enamored with the description of the ideal wife given in Proverbs 31. What a woman! Loving husbands, though, will not hold their wives to that high a standard.

5. *The final need of the husband is for admiration.* Male ego is famously

fragile. If wives need constant affection, husbands need constant reassurance. It's a tough world out there, and when a husband leaves home to face it, he needs to know that somebody believes in him. His wife can give that support by telling him how wonderful he is and how she has confidence in his abilities. This inoculates him against the temptation of other women he may meet who will tell him how great he is. Wise wives will never tear down their husbands with criticism about their personal characteristics—not even in private, and certainly not in public. Dwight says that "behind every man should be an admiring wife."

So there you have it: the secret of how the Nelsons overcame early difficulties to build a beautiful, satisfying marriage. As Dwight consciously strives to meet Karen's needs, and she studies how to meet his needs, they have grown into the type of partnership that many couples would envy.

But the good news is that such a marriage is available to everybody. The Nelsons suggest that the process can be neatly summed up in Ephesians 5:33: "Each of you, however, should love his wife as himself, and [each] wife should respect her husband" (NRSV).

Chapter 3

THE COUPLE THAT PRAYS TOGETHER . . .

Margaret and Larry's Story

A special issue of *Adventist Review* included articles on how to build a stronger marriage. A few weeks later the Letters to the Editor column featured some responses to the issue. One letter grabbed our attention: Everyone had told them their marriage could never work because of the great difference in their ages; they were hopelessly incompatible. Yet after 31 years their love was still burning brightly. Their secret? They love the Lord and worship Him together every morning and evening.

We knew the couple who wrote that letter. They had lived in our community and had both taught at Andrews University some years before. So we wrote to them immediately, and, to our delight, they agreed to share their adventure together in this book.

Margaret Roelke McNitt is a retired registered nurse who spent eight years working in hospitals in India, Burma, Pakistan, and Nigeria and 13 years at Washington Adventist Hospital in Maryland. She taught seven years in the Nursing Department at Andrews University. Larry McNitt received a Ph.D. in business administration from the University of North Carolina and taught at the University of Maryland and at Andrews University. For the past 16 years he has been teaching at the College of Charleston in Charleston, South Carolina.

MARGARET TELLS THE STORY

"Who is he?" I whispered to my friend at church.

"A professor at the University of Maryland."

"What's wrong with him?"

"He's too young."

Any thought of a possible romance vanished as quickly as it had come. I had just returned to my home church after four years as a nurse in the Seventh-day Adventist hospital in Karachi, Pakistan. Larry, the "too young" professor, was in the Sabbath school class that I taught. And in addition to being too young, Larry was also too quiet. Our communication consisted of benign smiles and some very sterile "good mornings" at church for the next two and a half years. Neither of us thought of the other as a candidate for romance.

One evening as I arrived early for a school board meeting, Bob Skeggs, the school principal, said, "Marg, who are you going to invite to the faculty-board banquet?"

In my most sarcastic voice I bantered, "Now, Bob, which *one* of my boyfriends would you suggest that I invite?"

Quick as a wink, he said, "I think you should invite Larry McNitt."

Without missing a beat I countered, "Oh, Bob, Larry is too young!"

"I don't think so, Marg," Bob argued.

"OK, Bob," I said with resignation in my voice, "I will invite Larry on one condition—that you come with us. I don't want a silent evening!"

The probability that Larry would refuse loomed large in my mind, so I chose to send my invitation by mail. To my happy surprise, he called to say that he would be happy to go with me. When Bob picked us up for the banquet, he had another couple with him. Larry and I sat in the back seat of the van and talked continuously during the 40-mile trip to and from the Peter Pan Inn.

When Larry passed the butter to me during the banquet, I said face-tiously, "Oh, no, I can't take the last pat of butter; that might make me an old maid!" We all laughed together, but Larry cut the butter in half, putting the first half on my plate, and the last half on his own plate.

As we drove home that night I talked about bicycling for exercise. A few days later Larry called to say that he had just bought a bike and would like to join me for exercise! We had some great times together along the old Chesapeake and Ohio Canal, picnicking, birding, and enjoying each other's company. But I never forgot the "too young" factor. How young is "too young"? Eight years? Ten years? Twelve years? Larry's hair was gray-ing noticeably; mine was still without a hint of gray. Naturally, I didn't want to ask Larry how "young" he was, and nothing that he said gave me a clue. He had completed his Ph.D. degree not long after his move to Maryland. I hoped that his studies could account for quite a few years. Spring gave way to summer, and summer to fall. Larry and I were obvi-ously enjoying each other's company, but the "too young" thought was al-ways in my mind.

One glorious autumn evening we were sitting in the swing at my home. Mustering all my courage, I said, "Larry, do you know how old I am?" In the course of teaching my Sabbath school class I had never tried to hide my age. Larry was a mathematician and statistician, so I was con-fident that he knew.

He answered quickly, "Yes, I know how old you are."

"How old am I?" I questioned.

"Fifty," Larry smiled as he replied.

"I am not!" I protested. "I am 49! But Larry, I have no idea how old you are."

"I was born in 1941," Larry said softly.

I burst into tears. I had been born in 1921. "Oh, Larry, I can't see you any more."

As I sobbed uncontrollably, Larry took me in his arms for the first time, trying to console me. I had even dared to dream that I would share the rest of my life with Larry. Now my dream was totally shattered. Our age difference was an impossible incompatibility. It could not be changed.

Through my tears I tried to reason with Larry, "You need to marry someone young enough to have children."

For some time neither of us said anything. I continued to cry. Finally Larry said, "Marg, if we do not marry each other, 10 years from now we may both be single and both be sorry."

Now, 31 years later—years filled with joy—we ask ourselves, "How could we find such joy, in spite of our impossible incompatibility?" The answer is a very simple one. In our morning and bedtime worship together we thank God daily for the gift of His love for us and for our love for each other. We ask Him to deepen, to strengthen, to purify our love in His love. And He has wonderfully answered!

Each morning as we finish our worship, we lie down on our bed facing each other with Kori, our long-haired Chihuahua, in Larry's arms. Looking into each other's eyes, we sing, "God is so good to us; He loves us so; He's coming soon."

Each Sabbath as we drive to church, I ask Larry, "Did I ever tell you . . . ?"

His eyes twinkle as he answers, "No, you never told me. Tell me."

I declare, "From the time I was a little girl I have always wanted my husband to take me to church with him."

Larry and I have always chosen to attend a small church. We have found great joy and strength in our church family and have always been actively involved. When Larry had a sabbatical from his teaching at the College of Charleston, he volunteered to teach at Spicer Adventist College in India. This strengthened our bond because it gave Larry an understanding of what I had experienced in overseas service in India, Burma, Pakistan, and Nigeria.

God has also strengthened another facet of our marriage. For years before we were married, Larry and I had each returned 10 percent tithe and had given an additional 10 percent for offerings. God has indeed "opened the windows of heaven" as we have continued this practice throughout our marriage.

At the moment Larry is revising the King James Version of the Bible in his daily time alone with God. I am merging—and memorizing—the Crucifixion scene, as recorded in the *Harmony of the Gospels,* with the account in *The Desire of Ages.*

We believe that by beholding Jesus we will become like Him. It is our goal to share Jesus' love and our love for each other forever. Imagine it! When my "too young" Larry is a trillion years old, I will be a trillion and twenty! God is so good to us!

Just a few weeks ago Sharon, a neighbor, was recounting a horrendous experience she had recently while white-water rafting in Nantahala Gorge. She was thrown under the raft and pinned between it and a huge boulder. She fought desperately to free herself for what seemed like an eternity. Her lungs burned as they cried out for air. She said, "Marg, I just knew that I was going to die."

Sixteen years ago Sharon and her family moved into our neighborhood, and we became good friends. One day Alana, Sharon's toddler, was with me in our backyard and suddenly said, "Jesus is dead."

I countered, "Oh, no, Alana; Jesus is not dead. He came out of the grave and lives in heaven. Jesus is alive and will be alive forever."

The following day Sharon came over and said, "Marg, please do not talk to our girls about Jesus or about God."

When Sharon finished her white-water rafting story, I had tears in my eyes. I said, "Sharon, I know that you don't believe in it, but for 16 years we have prayed for you and your family every day."

Sharon grabbed my arm and cried out, "Oh, Marg, that is wonderful!"

As we parted she put her hand on my arm and implored, "Please continue to pray for us."

Our dog, Kori, loves to "go along." Larry didn't think that I should take her with me to buy a few groceries, as it would be very hot in South Carolina's summer temperatures. I assured him that I would take only a few minutes and that I would open all the car windows while I was in the store.

When I came out of the store, I saw a police car blocking my car. I had not displayed my "handicapped" card. After I showed the police officer my card she said, "You will need to wait. You have two violations. You left your dog unattended. The animal control officer is on the way."

Both officers were very kind as I readily admitted that I was wrong on two counts. They very graciously forgave me for both offenses but reminded me that I could have been fined $200 for each one.

I was elated as I related my adventure to Larry, but was totally unprepared for his angry response. Such things don't usually upset him.

Only a few weeks earlier this same Larry said to me, very calmly, "Were you aware that you left the oven on broil for eight hours while we were out?"

I was horrified as I thought of what could have happened, but I thanked Larry for his patience with me. We sang our chorus, "God is so good to us," and thanked Him for saving our home from fire.

Larry's unexpected anger about my police encounters made me angry, and I retorted, "The police were far more understanding than you are." I banged the door loudly and went outside to lick my wounds. After a few minutes I came back in and said, "I'm sorry."

"I'm sorry, too," Larry said.

Even though we had made things right, I was still feeling hurt. Larry left for school, and I sat down with my Bible. I needed to find something that would tell Larry how deeply I was hurt, something that would encourage him to be more understanding. Nothing helpful came to my mind. I reached for a Bible promise box, asking God to give me a text that would help me. I could hardly believe the printed answer He gave me: "Now instead, you ought to forgive and comfort him, so that he will not be overwhelmed by excessive sorrow. I urge you, therefore, to reaffirm your love for him." In the margin of 2 Corinthians 2:7, 8, NIV, I wrote: "Police-Kori-Larry 7-11-01."

LARRY TELLS THE STORY

There are several things that we believe strengthen our marriage beyond normal expectations. By far the most important is that we are firmly committed to the Lord and to our church. We spend 30 to 40 minutes each day in morning and evening worship and prayer together. We also spend additional time in our private devotions.

Both of us paid tithe and gave additional offerings before we were married and continued that pattern after we were married. We love our church, support it financially, and invest our time in it. This reduces the stress on our marriage.

We have similar (old-fashioned) views regarding church standards and lifestyle issues. Neither of us smokes or drinks alcoholic beverages. We have similar tastes in music and entertainment. Neither of us watches television unless there is a national disaster or a hurricane threatens our coast.

Both of us believe in regular church attendance and in attending the mid-week service, as we both had done before we were married. Marg was amazed that I, a "young" person, came regularly to prayer meeting. Our spiritual commitment has strengthened our marriage as God has promised.

One of our more interesting adjustments involved our vehicles. When we were married, I drove a Ford van and Marg drove a sporty two-door Chevrolet. Her car had air-conditioning, automatic transmission, power steering, and power brakes. My van didn't have air-conditioning, automatic transmission, power steering, or power brakes. She complained that my van rode like a truck. Even so, she wanted to learn to drive my truck.

We found an empty parking lot for lesson number one. She hadn't used a manual transmission for years. She finally got it in first gear, and we started straight ahead. She twisted the steering wheel—and nothing happened. We were still going straight ahead. She pressed on the brake. Nothing happened. We continued coasting along. By putting both feet on the brake pedal, she slowed us to a stop, but there were not enough feet to push the clutch pedal as well. Thus ended Marg's first-and-only lesson in how to drive a truck.

We bought a camper van that did have air-conditioning, automatic transmission, power steering, and power brakes. Marg drove that occasionally, but she still said that it rode like a truck.

When we hold marriage seminars we offer several prescriptions that guarantee a lasting and happy marriage. The first of these is that the couple should pray together and for each other every day. God at the center of a home is a unifying force. Research has clearly shown that homes where regular family worship is conducted not only are homes with greater marital satisfaction but also homes that produce children who are more likely to remain in the church when they reach adulthood. The couple who pray together are the couple who stay together.

With God beside you, you can triumph through thick or thin.

Chapter 4

MAKING GOD THE CENTER OF THE MARRIAGE

Tena and George's Story

*N*o element is more crucial in making a success of marriage than putting God at the center of the relationship. "The couple that prays together stays together." Praying for each other, worshiping in the home and at the house of God, and serving Jesus for the benefit of humanity are the practices that bind a marriage solidly together through the years.

A marvelous illustration of this fact is found in the experience of our friends George and Tena Baehm. This is the story of a couple who overcame huge obstacles that began at birth, and how they continue to overcome so that they can serve others.

FACING THE GIANTS IN LIFE

To Tena and George, all of us must look like giants. Everything around them is gigantic, because everything is geared to the average person's height, which is much too high for them. George stands at four feet tall, and Tena at three feet and 10 inches. They call themselves "God's littlest sheep." Since their retirement they report that they rely on God to provide them with the strength to negotiate life's challenges and to live a life of service through volunteer ministries to the Seventh-day Adventist Church. One of their favorite Bible texts is "I can do all things through [Christ] who strengthens me" (Philippians 4:13, NRSV).

We first met Tena and George while we were on a tour of China. It was impressive to see how gracefully they dealt with stares, questions, and the everyday challenges of handling pieces of luggage that were as big as they were. In spite of this, they were continually looking for ways to share their faith with everyone they met, which caused some consternation for the Chinese Communist soldiers.

TENA TELLS THE STORY

We will never forget that day 38 years ago when we first met. It was at a Little Peoples' Conference (for short-statured people four feet, 10 inches and under) in Asheville, North Carolina. Both in our late 20s, we each wanted a life companion whose beliefs were centered on God. Also, we each wanted a mate who had similar physical conditions—dwarfism. Eye-to-eye contact can't happen when one person is six feet tall and the other is four feet tall. We were looking for a Prince Charming and a Princess with whom to live happily ever after. We were both praying that a miracle would happen. And it was a dream that God fulfilled!

Marriage is honorable (Hebrews 13:4). It was one of the first of God's gifts to humanity, and it is one of the few institutions that Adam brought with him beyond the gates of Paradise (see *Patriarchs and Prophets*, p. 46). Each of us has that desire for closeness, and instilled in us from the beginning is the longing to establish a home of our own. We are certainly thankful that God planned for us not to be alone as we realize that we would be lost without each other.

From the time we are born, all of us reach out for someone to love us and for someone to cherish. Love is vital in today's challenging society. When love is missing, humans may lose the will to live, and fatal illness can often result. When we experience this love from each other we glow with radiance and feel secure. This intimacy affects us physically, mentally, socially, and spiritually. It is the most wonderful thing that has happened to us. Here are the secrets of our happy marriage:

Praying alone and with my mate. We begin each day with God, first privately and then together. We pray for each other, asking for strength and guidance in our marriage. We have found that we must make a commitment to follow God's will for our lives each day, even if we don't always understand His plan for us. He will then guide our emotions, and eventually we will sense His presence. According to the divine plan marriage means having a relationship between two persons that becomes a three-sided relationship consisting of husband, wife, and God. As husband and wife we draw closer to God and certainly closer to each other.

It is also important for us to participate in public worship together. That was a dream of mine that was fulfilled. I envisioned my mate sitting beside me in the Adventist church—singing, worshiping, praising God, and participating together. Both of us are now deacons and greeters. We also are active in Sabbath school. Praying and worshiping together keeps the marriage on the right track.

Hospital times. In spite of good overall health, both of us have had surgery at different times. Those separations became difficult for us. In 1982 George had to have a hip replacement at Johns Hopkins Hospital. I was fortunate that I could be with him during his stay there. A friend on the hospital staff invited me into her home, so I was able to go to the medical center each day and be with him.

All the prep work had been done the day before his surgery. I was able to spend a couple of minutes with him, and we prayed together. It was so comforting to know that while we had a very competent physician, we knew that we also had the Great Physician who would be guiding the surgeon's hands. Both of us had great faith. It had been the same for me when I had to have major surgery earlier. George was able to stay with me for the first few days before he had to return to New York to attend to business. Both of us made a full recovery.

Patience when things get rocky. On occasions George would get angry at me, and I didn't know why. In a few seconds it was over, but I felt I had been insulted and terribly hurt. Sometimes those incidents arose as he worked in the family business and his father would get upset with him.

Afterward, I received the anger from George. When I asked about it later, he was apologetic, saying it was something he didn't get a chance to take care of when his dad had given him an extra responsibility. He said that he was sorry and that we should forget it. (I must share here that a week after our honeymoon I began working in the family business.)

When I look back at the experience, I don't know how our marriage survived! During those 27 years we had a one-week vacation during which George would have to keep in touch with his dad by phone about the business, no matter where we were. I really felt I was mistreated as an in-law. But now, after those 27 years, I am so thankful that I supported George during that crisis. We still have each other and are happier than ever

Supporting my mate, whatever the crisis, pays off in the end. Remember you are married, and don't let the family interfere with your marriage. We wives are more sensitive to feelings than our husbands. Yes, there are times when there are reasons for impatience—stress from the job, fatigue, or past irritations. Several times I've told George that I'll forgive him if he'll forgive what I have done. We make up with a hug and a kiss. Sometimes these little incidences make for a stronger marriage. George always says, "Let's kiss and make up."

Joint decisions. We've learned to discuss decisions, especially future plans. When someone from church calls and invites us to their home for a party or a meal, we discuss it. If we both agree, it's OK. So remember, wives, husbands don't like you to make plans without their input. Usually they will assent to whatever it is. We wives need to find out what makes our mates happy and what makes them unhappy. Of course, that works both ways. There are many challenges in marriage, and Satan is there to destroy it if he can.

Accepting your mate. George was not an Adventist when we met, but he was a very sincere Christian, active in his local church as an elder. Being a happy girl growing up in Minnesota, attending a self-supporting school in Wisconsin, and later studying at Southern Missionary College in Tennessee, I was brought up to dress modestly and with simplicity. I wore no makeup—was just plain and natural.

George chose me out of 75 women who happened to be at that Little Peoples' conference. He told me, "I like you just the way you are; you are everything I have pictured in my dreams." We need to tell our mates that we accept them just as they are. We can appreciate their unique habits and assure them that we are not out to change their characteristics.

George and I discussed some of our dislikes. It annoys George if I file my nails when he's around, so I try not to do that. I'd like him to be neater by not leaving things lying around, picking up his clothes, and not saving things that aren't important. I must say, he's improving, and he can understand my views on these things. I try to mention concerns in a loving manner that would encourage our relationship. Husbands need to have an area that is theirs, such as their desk, where they can arrange things without wifely interference. So I try not to nag about these areas, and concentrate on his better points. Nagging won't change anything; it just aggravates the situation.

Laughter and joyfulness. We've discovered that it's important to cultivate happy dispositions, to share funny things that take place during the day—and to laugh a lot. Cheer each other up. Look on the positive side of life. Laughter is a wonderful tranquilizer for problems. Learn how to laugh and make merry over mistakes. When we do this, a wonderful transformation takes place in the home.

We love to go grocery shopping together, meeting people in the fresh fruit and vegetable aisles. How thankful we are for the health message! We enjoy going up and down the aisles selecting the food items, especially cereal. The most healthy and nonsugar products are on the top shelves. Always. So we must wait until someone comes along who can assist us in reaching for a particular item. We say, "Do you always shop here on Tuesdays?" They catch on and reply, "Well, we'll see you again next week on this day!" We leave our new friend with a chuckle and often hear him or her comment, "I noticed all the healthy things you have in your shopping cart." We explain that we are vegetarians and share how this lifestyle has resulted in excellent health.

Great moments in our lives. George spent two years attending the Adventist church, studying with various pastors and evangelists. My family and I were praying that one day soon the Holy Spirit would touch George's heart with God's last-day message. On January 27, 1990— George's birthday—we were both baptized. I had drifted away and was so thankful to come back. The pastor suggested that it would be nice to be baptized together. The Lord answered many prayers, and now we felt equally yoked. During those many years I had been attending George's Sundaykeeping church; however, I knew in my heart that that was neither the day nor the truth.

Renewing our vows. We had been married in George's church. I had always longed to have a wedding performed in an Adventist church with an Adventist pastor officiating. On our thirtieth anniversary we renewed our vows. A candlelight wedding was held in the Old Westbury Seventh-day Adventist Church. Special invitations were sent out. Our niece and nephew from California were the attendants. My sister, Esther, from California accompanied the organist on the piano. Two Korean sisters were the flower girls. There were two Bible boys, a Korean and a Romanian. A Korean quartet had the special music, and a Korean friend played "The Lord's Prayer" on the violin. During the lighting of the unity candle we sang to each other, "My Love I Give to You." Pastor Ron Wooten made it very personal by sitting on a stool in front of us. (He was the same pastor who had baptized us a couple years earlier.) This relieved the two of us from having to look up at him, and he did not have to look down at us. He told about our lives. A reception followed the ceremony in the fellowship hall. After that we took our relatives on our honeymoon to Israel. It was such a beautiful occasion!

I suggest that couples renew their vows at some point in their marriage, when they are older and more fully realize their total commitment to each other. It doesn't have to be a big fancy affair. We had fun planning ours with the help of our pastor and his wife, who was the coordinator. Please don't wait until you have been married 40 or 50 years. Repeating your vows to one another really bonds you together.

Oh yes, I might add that I wore my original wedding dress! I never dreamed I would get two uses out of it, since we have no children who might use it someday. (However, we do have two girls, 4 and 13, that we support who are in Hogar Escuela Adventist Orphanage in El Salvador. The oldest was baptized two years ago.)

Our dreams were fulfilled by our spiritual rebirth and by our marriage before God. We still have obstacles to face daily, but with God as the center of our marriage we can win the battle.

Joy of serving others. During the past six years we have become involved with Maranatha Volunteers International. We have traveled to many places of the world—India, Nepal, Argentina, Africa, Australia, Venezuela, Honduras, Panama, etc.—to use our small hands for God in the building of churches, schools, orphanages, and health clinics.

Most of these trips have been to developing countries, where they had shacks in which to worship. When we left, they had beautiful buildings, filled to capacity. In helping others we have received such blessings! We know God has a purpose for us to fulfill in life. Meeting other couples who enjoy engaging in this same type of effort, as well as sharing stories of how God has enriched their lives and their marriages, has helped us grow.

What a thrill to make a difference in someone else's life! I urge couples to get involved in this type of program. There is a place for each of us to share this message. It is so exciting to help build. Don't worry if you don't have experience; you will get it when you arrive. Jesus wants us to have an abundant life that is filled with joy, and He has demonstrated that this is possible only when we become involved in serving others. To have that opportunity to witness and to work with others of another culture can indeed be a joyful experience. We come home truly blessed, and that is why we love going again and again. We have been on 30 projects and want to keep going as long as we can. Today we are stronger than ever in the Lord's love and in our love for each other and for others.

Result. The complete marriage is the ability to enjoy one another, to have fun with one another, to laugh and find delight in one another's presence. The benefits of working together and the efforts to accomplish this cooperation will outweigh the struggles that may come. We are counting the blessings that God has showered upon us and praising Him for giving us mutual companions to be our lovers for the rest of our lives.

❖   ❖   ❖

George and Tena's story illustrates so well the likelihood of attaining a happy and lasting marriage, regardless of the circumstances, if we will put God at the center of our marriages and unite to serve Him and advance His mission in this world.

Chapter 5

CELEBRATING OUR
DIFFERENCES

Karen and Ron's/Melissa and Ken's Stories

*O*pposites attract. That's an old stock cliché. But guess what? It contains a lot of truth. We humans tend to see in others the desirable traits we lack in ourselves. We instinctively sense that if we can only attach ourselves to those admired by others we may develop some of the same beneficial qualities ourselves.

So opposites often marry. Cholerics select phlegmatics for their calm, laid-back, got-it-all-together personalities. Phlegmatics admire the cholerics' ability to get things done and succeed in the world. Sanguines see in melancholies the order and organization in their lives that they themselves do not possess. Melancholies are taken with the spontaneity and social graces of the sanguines. How wonderful to be the life of the party!

But the attraction can turn into a distraction. After a while the attributes one so admired in the other can grow old. That which seemed charming now gets on one's nerves. His excessive talkativeness at social events embarrasses her. He wonders why she doesn't get more done in a day. The differences become irritating. But here they are—stuck together for life! It seems more like a sentence than a celebration.

Nevertheless, some couples who are very different from each other have learned to adjust and achieve a happy marriage. They have learned even to appreciate their differentness and to celebrate their distinctive qualities. In this chapter we wish to illustrate this achievement with the stories of two special couples.

The first couple is Karen and Ron Flowers, codirectors of the Department of Family Ministries at the General Conference of Seventh-day Adventists. We are blessed to count them as good friends. Perhaps no other couple in Adventism has more expertise in marriage enhancement, parenting, and other family life ministries. They have traveled the world holding various seminars on how to build viable Christian homes and have prepared a long collection of materials on the family for use in sermons, seminars, and individual homes. However, it wasn't always that way. Here is their story.

KAREN AND RON FLOWERS: CELEBRATING OUR DIFFERENCES

Early in our marriage, when viewing test results that revealed differentness that bordered on polarization on nearly every front, Ron blurted out: "I'm afraid this marriage may self-destruct!" (Only 5 percent of couples who are as different as we are remain together.) And true to his concern, we have discovered that facing our differentness and working through the issues it creates have been among our most significant marital challenges.

We knew we were different; that wasn't a surprise. Karen had never met anyone who could get more done in a day than Ron. What she didn't know was the extent of Ron's agenda and how hard it would be to put bounds on work. Ron admired Karen's spontaneity. What he didn't know was how frustrating she could be when she wanted to overturn his carefully laid plans at the last minute. Karen loved Ron's fix-it abilities. What she didn't know was that keeping things functional was sufficient for him; aesthetics mattered little. Ron loved Karen's openness. What he didn't know was that she would knock so incessantly on the closed doors of his past—doors he wanted to forget and had never planned to open to anyone. And on and on.

In addition to our personal differences, we, like all couples, brought to our marriage a "suitcase" filled with the bits and pieces of life that made up our understanding, as well as our hopes and dreams of what our marriage would be like. Karen came from a home that placed a high value on identifying and using the strengths of each member of the family, with little concern about maintaining traditional roles. For example, it was not at all unusual to find her mom at the table writing checks for the bills while her dad cooked supper.

Ron, on the other hand, came from a family where his mother was in charge of everything *inside* the house, and his dad was in charge of everything *outside* the house. So set were their roles that Ron remembers delivering the fresh milk from the barn to the doorstep, where his mother retrieved it and brought it inside the house to put it through the cream separator. Task completed, his mother returned it, now in two cans, to the doorstep, where his dad took over again.

So Karen and Ron get married, both with clear ideas about what marriage is all about—until the first evening when Ron waits patiently for dinner, and Karen, caught up in one of her projects, assumes Ron will get something going in the kitchen when he's hungry.

Growth toward celebrating our differences has defined in large measure the journey of our life together. At first we pretended we weren't really all that different, each so intent on maintaining honeymoon bliss that we were willing to give in to the other on any front. But as the rub produced more and more irritation, we changed tack and both diligently set about to change the other.

Ron provided every possible tool to get Karen organized—to no avail. Karen jumped into the harness with Ron, convinced that if she helped him complete his agenda there would be more time for play. But the agenda only grew in proportion to her efforts. Ron heard Karen's not-so-subtle hints for love gifts and, in keeping with his practical nature, bought her an artificial flower arrangement with little attention to decor. Karen responded by selling the arrangement at a yard sale. The stage was set for deep hurt and much trouble. Fortunately, a strong love bond and commitment to each other and marriage led us to seek the path of growth.

Across our marriage two avenues have converged that have made all the difference. The first is our growing understanding of the gospel and its call to reflect God's agape love in our relationships with each other. Some of the most intimate and precious moments we have enjoyed together have been times when the implications of the words of Scripture have broken through at the most practical level on our marriage. We have acknowledged our powerlessness to become one in our own strength. And we have basked in the good news that God has brought us together in Christ (1 Corinthians 1:30), broken down all the barriers that divide us, and become our peace (Ephesians 2:14). Our oneness is not of our own making. It is His gift. We can learn only to unclasp our fists to receive it.

Alongside this wonderful news, we have actively sought to learn from other couples and develop relational skills that would enable us to treat one another with respect and find solutions to our challenges that were mutually acceptable and satisfying. The path of growth is never linear. It's more like two steps forward and one step back. But a replay of our intentional journey toward mutuality, love, and intimacy reveals encouraging progress and provides courage for the next step.

Not long ago we found ourselves with a couple of days between appointments, perched on the edge of Yellowstone National Park. With delight we headed for the entrance to this place we had always dreamed of visiting but, predictably, with two very different ideas about how to get the most out of two days in a place where you'd like to spend a month.

It was springtime, and everything was in bloom and had babies. Karen would have been content to spend the entire two days in the meadow just beyond the visitors' center, keying out wild flowers and new Western birds to add to her life list. Ron wanted a map. In two days, he told himself, you could surely get around and "conquer" the place. Ron's vision came complete with a minute-by-minute plan. Karen's vision could only unfold like the wonders before her. Neither had said anything to the other about what the next two days might hold.

Stopping by the gift shop at the visitors' center while waiting for the next predicted eruption of Old Faithful, we drifted apart from one another, meeting some time later at the cash register. We both held something behind our backs to purchase. As hands came around to place the chosen purchases on the counter, Ron, with a smile, produced local wild-flower and bird guides, while Karen winked and brought forward a map. It was a very special moment of celebration as each offered the next two days to the other as a gift of love.

We have made the journey from acknowledging and accepting our differences, to tolerance and respect. We now foray more and more often into the experience of actually enjoying this very different person who is our life mate, even treasuring the differentness that once threatened our life together. Certainly we have learned that our differences are often complementary. For sure, our life together has never been dull! We are very thankful to God for His reconciling work in Jesus Christ and His power at work in our marriage and to many fellow pilgrims who have shared their marriage journey and life lessons with us. Yes, we experience the pain of brokenness in our relationship. But, praise God, we also know the beauties of grace, forgiveness, and beginning again. It is cause for celebration!

◆　◆　◆

The second couple to share their story is Ken and Melissa Hanson. Melissa Sexson Hanson suffered through the experience of having two pregnancies miscarry. Out of her grief she authored a book to help other parents deal with this situation. *I Can't Find a Heartbeat: Hope and Help for Those Who Have Lost an Unborn Child* was recently published by the Review and Herald Publishing Association. Melissa lives in Kansas with husband, Ken, and their three children, Matthew, Jonathan, and Krista. Their marriage story is told in her voice.

MELISSA SEXSON HANSON: HEADS OR TAILS

"I have loved you with an everlasting love; I have drawn you with loving-kindness" (Jeremiah 31:3, NIV).

After 13 years of marriage I have discovered that happiness in a relationship can be as unpredictable as a flip of a coin. Heads, our marriage is great; tails, it's rotten. I'm sure that God never intended any relationship to be tossed to and fro by mere luck. So for years I struggled to determine the secret of true contentment in my marriage, fearing my chances were about as good as winning the lottery.

On one particular "tails" day, I asked Ken how he felt our marriage was going. He looked me straight in the eye and replied, "Our relation-ship seems to revolve around what mood you are in." For some reason his response haunted me like an overdue bill. The more I tried to ignore it, the more urgent it became. I felt God tugging at my angry heart, but stub-bornly I resisted. After all, I had plenty to resent.

For instance, Ken was supposed to finish building a fence for our back-yard. With two small children a fence was more than just a casual want; it was a safety issue. However, Ken always came up with some excuse to work on something that I felt was less pressing. After I had several months for its completion, my patience expired and my anger boiled. As I sat down for my worship I began emptying out my frustrations on God. Why didn't He change Ken? I knew He had the power. I had certainly prayed hard enough that He would. So why wasn't He answering my prayers? If only Ken wasn't so unreliable. When *I* said that I would do something, I always did it. Why couldn't he be more like me. *More like me?*

And then it hit me. The cold hard truth. I was dependable, all right, but rather monotonous. In all honesty, one of the things I admired most about Ken was his spontaneity. For example, when we got engaged we hopped in the car and drove all night to tell his folks in person. Ken's idea, of course. And then there were the flowers. They came when I least ex-pected them, even when no birthday or anniversary was in sight. If he were more "dependable," like me, would he be as fun-loving? Could it be that the character "faults" that irritated me most about Ken were the flip-side of the ones I loved the most?

As the reality of this truth stacked up in my mind, I stored it away as one of my priceless treasures. God accepted my weaknesses as well as my strengths and loved me with an "everlasting love." Perhaps I could apply His strategy on my husband. Then our marital happiness would no longer be dependent on a mere toss of the coin. It would be safe in God's bank account.

❖ ❖ ❖

Two couples—each with two mates widely different from each other. How can couples with such extremely diverse personalities ever make a marriage flourish?

In the case of the Flowerses, they came to a fuller understanding of the gospel of grace. If God loves us dearly in spite of our sins and rebellion, surely we can love others in spite of their faults. If God's beneficence is not predicted on our living up to some standard (Matthew 5:44-48), should we put conditions on our love for our mates? The Flowerses were also willing to be mentored by other couples who had worked out satisfactory ways of relating. They studied to learn human relationship skills and put them into practice. Finally, they each decided to think of the other's needs before their own, as the touching Yellowstone Park story reveals.

In Melissa's case it was a moment of insight. As we all must do, she recognized that while her spouse was not perfect, neither was she. Can we who are less than faultless expect perfection in our mates or other family members with whom we relate? She discovered that when we are filled with the love of God, we find it natural to love others—even our flawed spouses.

The common theme here is coming to appreciate the distinctive qualities of our partners. Would we really want another person to be just like us. Someone has said that if two people agree on everything, one of them isn't necessary. Each brings his or her unique strengths to the marriage. The key to a happy marriage between two opposites is learning to value—even celebrate—each other's qualities.

Chapter 6

MARS AND VENUS IN ACTION

Anonymous Couple's Story

John Gray's book *Men Are From Mars; Women Are From Venus* has been wildly popular because it touches on a fundamental but often overlooked truth: *Men and women are different!* And isn't that great? Most men would not wish to marry another man, and most women would not want to marry another woman. We are attracted to opposites. Yes, men and women are different, and, as the French say, *vive la différence!*

Having established that essential point, however, we must immediately note that the situation is fraught with complications. Why does this desirable reality cause so many problems? *Because we don't understand each other.* Men wonder why women don't think as they do. Women wonder why men don't feel as they do. It would make life so much simpler if we were on the same page. In the musical *My Fair Lady,* Henry Higgins, the consummate chauvinist, laments in a song, "Why can't a woman be more like a man?"

Making an effort to understand our spouses is one of the most important skills in attaining a great marital relationship. Beyond mere understanding, husbands and wives must *allow* their partners to be themselves—to have different personalities, different ways of thinking, different styles of doing. Ellen White once wrote, "Neither the husband nor the wife should attempt to exercise over the other an arbitrary control. Do not try to compel each other to yield to your wishes. You cannot do this and retain each other's love" (*The Ministry of Healing,* p. 361).

Even more, if we would build happy, satisfying relationships we will not only attempt to understand our mates and allow them to be their unique selves; we will *celebrate* our differences. We will rejoice for the richness that differing perspectives brings into our lives together. "Often [husbands and wives] discern in each other unsuspected weaknesses and defects; but the hearts that love has united will discern excellencies also heretofore unknown. Let all seek to discover the excellencies rather than the defects" (*ibid.*, p. 360).

The following experience illustrates these differences and how to deal with them. Given their Asian culture and sensitive natures, this couple has asked to remain anonymous. The husband has held important positions in Adventist higher education and presently serves as an executive in one of the world divisions of the Adventist Church. The wife is a homemaker who is involved in a number of ministries. She is the narrator of their special marriage story.

My husband and I have been married for 27 years. Our personalities are very different. Even though we are both from the same Asian culture (Chinese), we were brought up with different backgrounds, views, and customs. Especially difficult and lonely were the years when my husband was pursuing doctoral studies while preparing for the teaching ministry in an overseas mission, and when he was later employed as one of the administrators in an overseas educational institution. With the many stresses bombarding him each day at work, there were times when there was complete "silence" at home and some insensitive words spoken (with no intent to hurt). He was so engrossed in his work that there was not much private time for us.

I was looking inward, feeling sorry for myself, and wanting his attention. I felt that he was insensitive to my emotional needs and my lonely feelings. The turning point came one day when I opened up to him about how I felt. The Lord was good. He answered my prayers. He saw the emotional hurt that was in me and worked things out in such a wonderful way!

One day my husband invited me to conduct a Marriage Enrichment seminar with him and to prepare by reading books on marriage. That opened my eyes even further about marriage and my life partner. In our presentation, I focused on understanding men, while he focused on understanding women.

While helping others, I was blessed. The books *MEN: A Woman's Guide to Understanding a Man,* by Chuck Snyder (1995), and *Men Are From Mars; Women Are From Venus,* by John Gray (1992), were excellent resources in my preparation. Some of the things I found helpful to know about men are:

- Men are goal-oriented; women are relationship-oriented.
- After marriage, men's first love is their work.
- Men won't stop and ask for directions.
- Men can't pick a television channel and stay on it.
- Men do not put the toilet seat down.
- Men are more one-dimensional and focused; women are multiaware.
- Men go into the "cave" when they are under stress. They become increasingly focused and withdrawn. Men feel better by solving problems by themselves. Men pull away and think things out. Women feel better just talking about the problems and thinking out loud.

How to Support Him When He's in the "Cave"

- Don't try to help him solve his problem by offering solutions.
- Don't try to nurture him by asking questions about his feelings.
- Don't sit next to the door of the cave and wait for him to come out. Instead, do something to nurture yourself, such as reading a book, exercising, or giving yourself a treat.

Men's Five Most Basic Needs in Marriage

- Sexual fulfillment (highest need).
- Recreational companionship.
- An attractive spouse.
- Domestic support.
- Admiration.

Men see love as being a good provider, having sexual relations, fixing things around the house, and just being together. Women see these as only routine necessities of life.

Women's Five Most Basic Needs in Marriage

- Affection (highest need).
- Conversation.
- Honesty and openness.
- Financial support.
- Family commitment.

Being a committed Christian, my husband began to see to it that he would involve me as much as possible so we could spend more time together. Also, he was willing to say SORRY when I told him he hurt me.

Here are some of the things I learned to do that have improved our marriage:

I try to settle family conflicts or squabbles before nightfall. Knowing my partner's personality traits is very important. I now realize that the way he behaves is closely associated with his personality traits and family background.

Having a positive view of my self-worth is important. I respect myself. In return others, including my spouse, are much more likely to respect me. Reciprocally, I respect him for the way he is and do not try to change him. I make an effort to focus on his good points rather than his bad points. I want to help him become all he can be. Behind every successful man is a supportive woman.

We work on accepting each other's differences and try not to take the areas in which we disagree too seriously. Another goal is to have a sense of humor and to always be happy and cheerful. At all times, we want to rejoice in every little thing. We want to be aware of each other's needs and learn how to meet them. We try to allow the other person to be who he or she is.

Finally, it is so important to keep our love burning—I love him with all my heart, and love is contagious! And most important, I invite Christ into our home each day.

◆　◆　◆

This wife's summary contains a wealth of wisdom for those who are coping with differing personalities and styles of relating. A key initiative is to accept one's mate as being a separate, unique person with habits and manners that may be different from one's own but that, nevertheless, are a valid way of living for that person. I must always keep in mind that *my partner does not have to be a carbon copy of me.* In fact, my marriage will be much more interesting and satisfying when it includes both of our perspectives.

And don't overlook the theme of the committed Christian life to which she refers several times. Having God at the center of our homes helps us to work through differences that might otherwise appear insurmountable.

Chapter 7

JOB VERSUS FAMILY

The Oliver Family Story

*I*t can happen to any couple, but professional people and those with demanding, no-set-hours occupations are especially vulnerable. They may have married young before obtaining much higher education and are somewhat equal in their level of preparation. But then one of them—usually, but not always, the husband—continues to develop professionally. He may take graduate-level education or other professional preparation. As he gains experience and tenure, he begins to rise in whatever hierarchy in which he is employed. He becomes increasingly more successful, and the added responsibility requires him to spend more and more time in his vocation, and less time with home and family.

Meanwhile, the wife may be stuck back at square one. She has devoted her life to helping her husband through school, supporting him in his profession, taking care of the children, and keeping up the household. As the gap widens between them, she feels left behind. Her husband has won accolades for his work, but she doesn't get much recognition for vacuuming carpets, doing dishes, and diapering kids. She'd like to have a career of her own, to make her place in the world, not to have to always play second fiddle.

This situation can put a major strain on the marriage, and many couples don't make it. Divorce becomes the attempted solution. It is possible to transform this plight, however. It is possible to work through this impasse and find creative solutions. With God's help, it is possible to turn lemons into lemonade.

Let us introduce you to a couple who have gone through the trauma of "job versus family" and survived. Elaine and Willie Oliver are an amazing couple. Willie directs family ministries for the North American Division of Seventh-day Adventists. Elaine now has a part-time position as an assistant in that department, so they can work together. But it wasn't always that way. The Olivers show great courage and vulnerability in being willing to open up and share this very sensitive story. They do it in the hope that their experience will encourage readers who find themselves locked in the same vicious circle. There *is* a life beyond the job!

❖ ❖ ❖

ELAINE: Willie and I have always prided ourselves on having an egalitarian relationship. We've had mutual respect and support for one another's careers or calling from the beginning of our relationship. As we were both employed outside the home, we determined there would not be any division of labor according to gender but according to time and availability and, perhaps, some personal preference. (Willie doesn't do bathrooms, and I don't wash cars.) Compromise was not a dirty word in our vocabulary; we learned how to be accommodating of each other. Whoever arrived home first would prepare dinner; the other person would clean up afterward. Most times we'd clean up together because it was our way of spending time together and catching up on the events of the day.

This almost-seamless system continued even after the arrival of our children. I can honestly say that I was very spoiled. Willie attended every doctor's visit during our pregnancies, and woke up for every feeding to bring me the baby. We were not perfect, and certainly had our share of couple and parenting disagreements, but our system of balancing work, family, and home was nearly flawless.

We should have known that our comfortable system could not last forever. It all changed drastically when we accepted a call from the North American Division, where Willie became the director of the Department of Family Ministries. This was a huge disruption for us because we had barely unpacked the boxes from our move only two years before. In addition, we had to leave the comfort and convenience of living close to family, good friends, and work.

It was especially difficult for me, because it meant leaving all that was familiar. We were moving from the town in which I had grown up. We would be further than we had ever been from my aging grandmother with whom I am very close. It meant giving up a well-loved and fulfilling job with no employment prospects on the other side.

Nevertheless, we felt that God was leading us, and we trusted Him to provide for us. We knew it was going to be quite a transition but thought we would get over the hurdle and quickly settle back into life as usual. What we did not anticipate was how much more demanding this new position would be for Willie and how disruptive it would be to our family life

A few days after we had unloaded the moving truck at our new home, with many boxes still unpacked, Willie had to leave for a four-day trip to Alberta, Canada. As his job required ever more travel, our previously well-orchestrated system began to unravel. When Willie was away, it meant that all of the responsibilities that he had cared for were left on my shoulders. Things functioned much better when the two of us were around to carry the load.

I missed having Willie at home on a daily basis and began harboring feelings of anger and resentment. I spent much time worrying and thinking about the "what ifs." I was irritated by the fact that because I was the one left to manage the household and the kids by myself, with no family or close friendships established yet, there was little time left for me to find a job. I wanted to be supportive of Willie's ministry but resented the disruption to our family life and to my career. I became very defensive and bitter in my interactions with Willie. The tension in our relationship began to escalate.

WILLIE: For my part, I was feeling the pressure of the need to adapt to the multiple demands of my new position yet remain connected to my family. I began to feel that Elaine was being unsupportive of me and was feeling frustrated at having to deal with so much tension at home while dealing with my most demanding job ever. Our financial picture was also very bleak because of changing from two-incomes to a single-paycheck budget. That added even more pressure to the situation.

Unfortunately, we didn't spend a lot of time sharing our feelings with each other. We found ourselves miscommunicating and arguing a great deal of our time. If truth be told we were both dealing with so many transitional issues that neither one of us had really taken the time to identify what our true feelings were. It was all so new to us that it took us a while to dig beneath the surface to find the hidden issues with which we were dealing.

ELAINE: The more resentful and bitter I became toward Willie, the easier it was for him to work late and stay away from home.

WILLIE: The more I was away from home, the more angry Elaine became. The tension was so great between us that we could hardly stand to be in each other's presence. It became a vicious cycle for us, one that could have been very destructive had we not allowed God to intervene. And all of this, ironically, while I was trying to lead out in family ministries.

ELAINE: It all suddenly changed one day as Willie was preparing to leave for a trip. I found myself feeling very weak and unable to get out of bed. Willie asked if I was OK. I answered an honest no and managed to confess to him how lonely and sad I was feeling. He became very concerned and asked if I wanted him to stay with me, and I said yes.

WILLIE: It suddenly hit me hard that something was very wrong with Elaine and that attending to her was more important than anything else in the world that "needed" my attention. I immediately canceled my trip and told Elaine that I would stay for as long as she needed me, and until she was well enough to function properly—even if it meant canceling a few more trips.

We spent the day talking and praying together. We shared our true feelings with each other and really tried to understand each other's viewpoint. We also agreed that we would need to find outside help—other people whom we could trust and who could hold us accountable. It was very difficult for us, as it is for most pastoral couples, to share our problems with others, but we knew that it would be necessary in order for us to get past this hurdle.

ELAINE: I decided to see a Christian counselor, and Willie shared with a trusted colleague. We saw different people because we knew that at that juncture we both needed to be able to vent openly about our feelings without fear of rejection or retaliation. Once we understood our own true feelings, we were better able to communicate them to each other and to begin the process of mending the rift that had occurred in our relationship in just a few short weeks.

The first change we made was to get back into the habit of praying together each morning. When frequent travel disrupts one's daily life, it's very easy for each person to develop his or her own rituals, which continue even after the traveling person returns. We were nurturing our own individual devotional lives but not spending enough time surrendering as a couple to God.

The one-minute hug was reincorporated into our daily routine when we arrived at home in the evening, or at anytime, for that matter. This is an excellent way to easily reconnect and bond with one another after a short or prolonged absence. If not intentionally nurtured, oneness and intimacy will dissipate, and that is especially true for couples whose relationships are affected by frequent traveling.

WILLIE: As for the traveling, I established a policy that I would accept appointments to be away from home only two weekends out of every month. The other two weekends I would spend at home. I have scheduled family Sabbaths for every other weekend, which appear as real appointments on my calendar. After all, it didn't make sense to be on the road trying to save families when my own was falling apart. I also made it a point to speak on the telephone with Elaine and Jessica and Julian every day I was away from home. This allows us to remain connected and underscores the high priority each holds in the others' lives.

ELAINE: I agreed that I would try not to schedule any appointments or activities for myself or our children on the days that Willie would be returning from a trip or during the time he was home. This way he wouldn't feel as if he were being left out of our lives. We also established more intentional conversation times while Willie was traveling. Instead of simply talking about the kids and the events of the day, we began asking about each other's feelings, thoughts, and concerns.

We finally began to operate as a team again. We recognized that we had been fighting against each other instead of fighting as allies against the evil forces that were threatening our relationship. Yes, things are drastically different than they were with our well-oiled machinery of those earlier years, and we know that many hurdles lie ahead. Nevertheless, each challenge gives us an opportunity to grow much closer to each other and to have a much clearer picture of the oneness that God intends for us to have as married people (Genesis 2:24, 25). We know that no matter what circumstances change in our lives or what challenges we may face in the future we are allies—intimate allies.

◆ ◆ ◆

This next story is somewhat different, yet it focuses on the same problem—how to reconcile the husband's professional life with the wife's needs. Willie and Wilma Kirk Lee direct family ministries in the Southwestern Union Conference of Seventh-day Adventists. While both are very competent, Wilma has proved herself to be a professional in her own right.

◆ ◆ ◆

Our story can best be heard through our individual voices; so please hear "our" perspective by listening for the dynamics of Christ-covenanted marriage as displayed in our developing relationship.

WILLIE: Ministry families enjoy a privilege that few can ever understand or comprehend. Our families are also placed in situations of jeopardy and crisis for which only our Lord is able to provide with His sustaining and healing hands. When my wife and I married, little did we know the types of challenges we would be facing.

WILMA: Actually, I was quite intimidated by the prospect of being the *perfect pastor's wife*—whatever that was supposed to be. I was certain that *everyone* knew what my role was—except *me!* I just wanted to be the best "me" possible, and I wasn't certain that was enough. The mere thought of all the other expectations involved was unsettling. One of the things that I dreaded the most was moving from place to place.

WILLIE: After a successful pastoral ministry in New York City, our newly acquired marriage and family relationship-building skills would be tested. When we received a call to move to California, in the San Joaquin Valley, we knew that God was answering our prayers for the provision of a friendlier climate, socially and geographically, to raise a family of three children, 9 years old and under. The opportunity for an Adventist Christian education was available through a church school within 15 minutes of our home.

WILMA: I wasn't certain about a move across country. After all, I was accessible to my parents and everyone I had known all my life with only an extended car trip. California was like moving to another part of the world! Yet all the things that I lay before the Lord (without sharing with my husband) were accomplished, and we moved. It was a challenge to move to another culture and way of doing things. However, it was a blessing to our family, and the Lord used this opportunity for all of our growth and progress.

WILLIE: As Christian parents, we had covenanted with the Lord and each other that parenting and nurturing children at home was more important than any amount of income gained by both parents working outside the home. One of the challenges that comes with that decision is the mother of the children having to become the stay-at-home parent with no income source or identity of her own. Either she is the pastor's wife, or his children's mother. I could hear and feel these sentiments being expressed continuously. Quite frankly, I had no idea how to help resolve these issues. They don't teach or expose you to these life situations at the seminary. And I certainly did not hear them discussed in my home. The suffering servant mode was all I knew.

WILMA: Don't get me wrong. Being a cherished wife and a nurturing mother are worthy roles, but those roles are not necessarily for everyone. They have to do with where one finds one's self in life. I wasn't certain what I wanted to be "when I grew up," but I did know that I had to have something to do that was uniquely mine, so that I could be a charming, interesting, and challenging partner when our children sprouted their own wings and flew away. By temperament I'm not the suffering servant type, and that was quite a challenge in learning how to deal with such wide differences in personality and approaches to life. I don't know that there is a resolution to these situations. I just know that the Lord can make a difference.

WILLIE: Another area that consumes relational energy is the incompleteness of the wife/mother development through education or vocational preparedness. I had a desire to see my wife through the completion of her collegiate goals, knowing that she had made sacrifices for me to complete my graduate and seminary studies. Among the challenges of logistics and reassignment of roles and responsibilities are the financial needs of supporting three children and a wife while incurring tuition, fees, and books on an Adventist minister's salary! And when you move your wife around the country, it is next to impossible for her to build the type of vocational security that guarantees even consistent part-time employment.

WILMA: I did manage to acquire a bachelor's and a master's degree after we had young children. There were evenings when the children and I sat at the dining room table together doing homework. I could not have accomplished these goals without the support of a husband who did not think that cooking, cleaning, or doing laundry was women's work. I actually gave my husband a certificate when I got my bachelor's degree that acknowledged all the support that he had given me to accomplish my academic goals.

WILLIE: Throw all these together, add the expectations the local congregation and the conference officials have of the pastoral couple, and you have the makings for difficult and stressful times. For me, these were depressing conditions.

WILMA: I would like to say only that if congregations, conferences, and all the others who are so quick to determine what the *perfect pastor's wife* looks like would apply the golden rule, there would be much joy on both sides. Each pastor is different, and the wife of the pastor reflects his differences. Each pastor's wife has her own unique gifts that she is given by God to develop and use for the building of His kingdom. I will be held accountable to the Lord for what He has given me and for what I have done with His gifts. Maybe sometime I can share what I *really* think!

WILLE: Looking back, I have often considered what might have been— another ministry, family broken and dismantled, statistically and realistically. Only a deep faith, supportive families, and God's rich love in our marriage made the difference. Many times our oft-experienced dialog, unconditional acceptance, and love were the only threads that held us together emotionally. Much forgiveness was processed between us. I learned much, and I am still learning. Our study of the Word and our prayers for and with our children cemented our relationship with God. Supportive visits and phone calls from family thousands of miles away secured our identity and "belongingness." Longtime friends provided assurance and relational succor.

WILMA: I realize every day that I serve such a loving God that I can't help sharing that love with those He has allowed to be a part of my life. Patrick Henry Reardon puts it best: "Suppose for a moment that God began taking from us the many things for which we have failed to give thanks. Which of our limbs and faculties would be left? Would I still have my hands and my mind? And what about loved ones? If God were to take from me all those persons and things for which I have not given thanks, who or what would be left of me?"

OUR TESTIMONY: "Who shall separate us from the love of Christ? Shall trouble or hardship or persecution or famine or nakedness or danger or sword? As it is written: 'For your sake we face death all day long; we are considered as sheep to be slaughtered.' No, in all these things we are more than conquerors through him who loved us. For I am convinced that neither death nor life, neither angels nor demons, neither the present nor the future, nor any powers, neither height nor depth, nor anything else in all creation, will be able to separate us from the love of God that is in Christ Jesus our Lord" (Romans 8:35-39, NIV).

"And now these three remain: faith, hope and love. But the greatest of these is love" (1 Corinthians 13:13, NIV).

As the fairy tale goes, the rich, cultured prince marries the unlettered peasant girl, and they live happily forever after. Believe us, it's a fairy tale! It is very difficult to sustain a truly companionship marriage when wide differences in cultural backgrounds, education, and economic status separate the spouses. One of the secrets of surviving the strains of marital life and building a happy and fulfilling marriage is to equalize the differences between the couple.

In both of these stories it was necessary for the professional husband to understand his wife's needs and include her development in their lives together. Of course, this is also true of the professional wife who needs to make her husband feel valued.

Notice also the crucial place that the love of God played in helping these couples work through their difficulties. As we draw closer to God, we draw closer to each other. Seeking outside counsel can be an important component for recovering a marriage, as illustrated by the Olivers. Sometimes we are so enmeshed in the problem that we can't see clearly. A trusted Christian friend or counselor can help us sort out our mixed-up emotions and look at viable options.

The important lesson is this: no situation is hopeless *if* both partners are willing to set self aside and consider the needs of the other.

Chapter 8

THE SEESAW OF MARRIAGE

Katherine and Reger's Story

Traditional marriages were less complicated than partnership ones. Under the traditional structure the husband was the head of the house, managed the finances, and made most of the decisions. The couple lived where his work was located. Women were largely expected to stay at home, take care of the house, and raise the children. Husbands were dominant; wives, submissive. Furthermore, proponents of traditional marriage claimed that the Bible supported this structure. (Some still do.)

Some years ago an interesting advertisement appeared in major publications. Entitled "The Working Partnership of 1908 Worked," it featured a distinguished gentleman, dressed in formal Edwardian style, sitting in a straight-backed chair of the period. Beside him stood his rather harried-looking wife, surrounded by broom, mop and pail, home canning, laundry, and knitting. A list of her duties was given: fetched wood, stoked stove, prepared feasts, polished floors, beat rugs, hauled water, furrowed garden, weeded garden, harvested garden, canned food, organized pantry, buffed silver, baked treats, washed windows, washed dog, fed dog, did shopping, decorated rooms, swept walk, sewed clothes, mended clothes, scrubbed clothes, straightened attic, aired bedding, and managed budget.

On the other side of the page was a list of his duties: provided wherewithal and approved where withal went. The punch line of the ad was "Baby, you've come a long way."

Obviously the ad was greatly exaggerated, but it does carry some insight into the traditional marriage. And to be sure, wives in general have come a long way. As we wrote some years back, "a new breeze of freedom has been blowing. . . . One can sense the rising feelings of democracy and hear the cries for self-determination. . . . This new spirit of individual consciousness has not passed women by. . . . Women today are looking for a new role in marriage. They are no longer willing to play second fiddle. They are not content to find their fulfillment in ministering to a man's needs and providing for his convenience. They want equal partnership in the marriage and will settle for nothing less" (*Married and Glad of It* [Review and Herald, 1980], p. 24).

How does God feel about all this? We won't take the time or space to debate such a difficult theological issue. You might check Genesis 1:27, 28; Proverbs 31:10-31; and Galatians 3:28. But wherever you stand, gender equality has become a reality—at least in Western society. Couples, who wish a happy, successful marriage will have to learn how to deal with it.

Now, if two people marry, and they both agree on how their union will be structured—traditional or contemporary—the potential for problems is minimized. But what if they differ? Or what if both come from traditional backgrounds, but during the course of the marriage the wife decides she wants more voice in the decision-making process? This scenario has generated conflict in many a home. How can the couple work through it?

Our short story touches on these issues. The self-assured, knows-where-he's-going man marries the timid, inexperienced woman. Katherine and Reger Smith have been married for more than 50 years. They have a great marriage and a great partnership. Reger has served both as vice president for student affairs and as chair of the social work program at Andrews University. Katherine worked for 12 years as a dean of women at Andrews, and 11 years as a medical social worker. They have been joint first elders at the 3,000-member Pioneer Memorial church on the university campus. Now retired, they muse on the beginnings of their marriage.

❖ ❖ ❖

REGER: I got out of the Army and came back to my former home in Detroit in November 1946. My father, a graduate of Union College in Lincoln, Nebraska, had been called to pastor the newly formed Benton Harbor Lake Region church in southwest Michigan. I had been complaining to my father about my dissatisfaction with the Detroit girls I knew, and he mentioned to me that he had met the type of girl he thought I was looking for in the new Benton Harbor church. I told him I would certainly look her over when I returned to Emmanuel Missionary College (now Andrews University) in Berrien Springs the following January.

On the first Sabbath I attended the new church, I met Katherine. The next Sabbath I went back to church, talked with Katherine some more, and told her I was going to marry her.

I was a veteran of the United States Army and had, therefore, traveled extensively. I was a fourth-generation Adventist and a preacher's kid. I was 20 years old and had completed a year of college. I knew where I was going in life, was self-assured, and had an ego bigger than I was.

KATHERINE: My family had moved to Benton Harbor from Arkansas in 1945. In 1946, when I met Reger, I was 17 years old and a junior at Benton Harbor High School. I was a new Adventist, having come into the church through an evangelistic campaign held by a senior pastor and students from Emmanuel Missionary College. I didn't know what I was planning to do beyond high school and had given no serious thought to either college attendance or marriage.

The students from the college were very encouraging to this new believer and optimistic about my attending Emmanuel Missionary College. When Reger presented his ideas about what my future should be, I did not take too kindly to his plans. However, being a rather shy, timid person, I rather liked the assurance and confidence that he displayed and was impressed and awed by someone with such a strong personality. I needed someone who could make decisions, and he was so intelligent. His status as a college student and as our preacher's son was also impressive. He was a handsome young man, and all of the older women of the church were in his corner. My mother thought he "walked on water."

REGER: Katherine had a non-Adventist boyfriend when I first met her, but with pressure from me and from my supporters in the small church, she soon gave him up. For the next two years we dated exclusively and were together every weekend. After two years together I thought I was ready for marriage, but Katherine (I found out later) had more sense. I left her and dated a girl in another town for a few months. Then we got back together and did marry two years later, after I had taught church school for a year and she had attended Emmanuel Missionary College for a year.

When we married, Katherine felt that she did not need to learn to drive because I could take her anywhere she wanted to go. She expected me to make most of the decisions and seldom questioned my judgment. I enjoyed this dominance and gave her very limited control of any part of our relationship.

But in the next few years Katherine, the girl I had married, became more and more of a woman and began to question my decisions and balk at my dominance. We had many arguments and disagreeable stalemates as I gradually learned to allow, expect, and even to admire her initiative and her independence. It took me years to learn that the more she contributed of herself to the relationship, the more woman I had to love.

After 50 years the learning and the changes go on. I am still learning to accept her decisions, even though I might have been initially opposed to them. I usually end up genuinely accepting—and even admiring—them. Married bliss is not 100 percent predictable, as I at first wanted it to be, but active love turns even the unpredictable times of life into a joyous and fulfilling adventure.

❖　❖　❖

Couples have split over the dominant-submissive issue. How did the Smiths struggle through those early conflicts to survive—and even construct a beautiful relationship? Reger had to gradually learn that there are two individual persons in a marriage relationship. He had to come to recognize that Katherine had needs and goals of her own. He had to come to see that when Katherine developed her own personality and stood on equal status with him, their bond became stronger and more mutually satisfying.

Katherine, on the other hand, needed to take on responsibility for her own life. She needed to become a person in her own right and not simply a mirror reflection of her husband. She had to learn to assert herself in a non-threatening way and help her husband to see her as an individual, not a trophy. For the mystery of marriage is that two people become one yet remain as two separate beings. As they develop themselves physically, mentally, emotionally, vocationally, and spiritually, they each have more to bring to their special relationship.

AND WHAT OF MARRIAGE?

Let there be spaces in your togetherness,
and let the winds of the heavens dance between you.
Love one another, but make not a bond of love;
let it rather be a moving sea between the shores of your souls.
Fill each other's cup, but drink not from one cup.
Give one another of your bread, but eat not from the same loaf.
Sing and dance together and be joyous, but let each one of you be alone.
Even as the strings of lute are alone though they quiver with the same music.
Give your hearts, but not into each other's keeping.
For only the hand of life can contain your hearts.
And stand together, yet not too near together:
for the pillars of the temple stand apart,
and the oak tree and the cypress grow not in each other's shadow.

—From Kahlil Gibran, *The Prophet*

Chapter 9

HOW TO KISS AND MAKE UP

The Valenzuela Family Story

W e've been married for 30 years and have never had an argument."
No, we didn't say that, but we've heard it said. One wit said
that when couples make a statement like that, it means one of two things:
either they have a very poor memory, or they lie.

Here's another one: If two people always agree on everything, one of
them isn't necessary.

Conflict is something that happens in all relationships, not just marital ones. Conflict can have a positive outcome if it results in a stronger relationship. As many of the stories in this book indicate, no two people
think alike in all things, or even appreciate and value the same things.
Conflict resolution is a topic that we've found many couples want to learn
more about when we hold marriage seminars. How can two people come

to a peaceful agreement when they don't see eye to eye? Let's examine some of the ways that conflict can be made into a positive experience.

PEGGY: This was a skill that I really needed to learn, because I did not learn it in my home. So when we first got married and I disagreed with Roger, I just withdrew into my silent self, because I didn't know how to voice my opinion in a way that would lend itself to peaceful resolution. During a Marriage Encounter weekend I heard a couple dialoging on this very topic, and suddenly my eyes were opened to some of the peaceful possibilities. This made such a difference in our marriage that we accepted an invitation to become marriage seminar facilitators.

Two couples sent us stories in which they mentioned how much help they received from attending marriage seminars. The first couple is Alfonso and Jeanine Valenzuela. Alfonso is a professor in the Christian Ministry Department and associate director of the Institute of Hispanic Studies, both at Andrews University. His doctorate is in family life studies. Jeanine is a nurse and homemaker.

We've been married for 25 years—25 beautiful years. Like most normal couples, we have had our downs as well as our ups. We think that if we have made it together during all these years it is because the ups have outnumbered the downs.

The first years were very difficult. We made the mistake most couples do when they get married—we weren't prepared for marriage. In those years premarital counseling wasn't available, or if it was available we didn't know about it. We're glad that today most churches don't marry couples unless they go through counseling sessions. We had the problems most couples have when they get married. We needed to be able to adjust to each other's unique personalities. We needed to learn how to communicate effectively. We had to work our way through financial difficulties.

Jeanine is from Puerto Rico, and Alfonso is from Mexico, so there were cross-cultural issues that we needed to understand if we wanted to adjust to each other. These things included food. In Puerto Rico they eat rice and beans every day; in Mexico they eat tortillas and beans with hot sauce. Each background has its idiomatic expressions. We both speak Spanish, but many words are totally different in their meaning in the two countries. We had to adjust not only to each other; we had to adjust to a new culture. (We came to the United States a year after we got married.) We had to adjust to a new type of work, a very stressful job. (We came to the U.S. to work for a church in Lincoln Heights, California.)

We soon realized that we needed to work on our communication skills if we wanted to stay together, so we made a serious decision to do something about the situation. We started spending more time together, talking about issues that were affecting our lives, such as Jeanine's work, the church, time together, and other concerns that were inundating us. One of the best things that really helped us was to go to a restaurant every week (like on a romantic date) and spend time just talking and being together. This is something we have done for the past 20 years.

Attending marriage encounter and enrichment programs has helped us tremendously. We try to attend one of these programs at least once a year. We have learned a lot from professional counselors and therapists, as well as from other couples who have attended those meetings.

What are the three most important elements for a happy marriage? We sat down and pondered that question. We finally agreed on what we consider the three most important ones: good communication, romanticism, and commitment to the relationship.

Last year we again met one of the couples, Antony and Elsebeth Butenko, who had attended our seminar several years previously. They had come to Andrews University from Sweden with their four children so that Antony, a pastor, could work on his Doctor of Ministry degree at the seminary. Antony and Elsebeth found the "knee-to-knee" exercise very useful, and at the time of our meeting a couple years later, they reported that they still continue to practice it. We asked if they would be willing to share their experience with our readers, which they graciously did. Antony is doing the reporting.

While attending one of your marriage seminars at the university, I asked this question: "What do you do when you have small problems that appear now and then in a marriage, and you can't seem to resolve them?" You didn't have the answer written in the marriage seminar manual, but what the two of you illustrated for us has been a tremendous help in our marriage.

When Elsebeth or I have a problem, we go into the bedroom and close the door. We sit on chairs, facing each other, so that our knees are touching, mine touching hers on the outside of her closed knees. We take each other's hands, look into each other's eyes, and reaffirm our love for each other. Then the one having the problem expresses how he or she feels now, or felt when the problem arose. We don't use any "you" words, only "I" words—"I feel such and such at this time."

Then we ask if the other one understands what the first one is trying to communicate. In each case the other spouse will listen carefully, without interruption, and reflect back the feeling that has been perceived, expressing sorrow for hurting the other. We again reaffirm our love for one another, and life goes on.

This event takes only five to 10 minutes and is a very valuable tool when both partners are working full-time and have four children to look after, three of whom are teenagers. Thank you for sharing this unique problem-solving tool with us!

❖ ❖ ❖

PEGGY: As I mentioned at the beginning of this chapter, I learned, while attending a Marriage Encounter weekend, that retreating into myself was not useful to the relationship. Roger didn't understand what was going on in my head, and for me nothing about what I was troubled changed because no one knew what was bothering me. Someone at the weekend said it was like pulling the window shade down in front of someone's face when that person is trying to see in.

I also learned that there are a number of reasons people use the "silent treatment," such as not knowing how to share feelings, hoping the problem will go away on its own (it seldom does), wanting to punish the other person with silence, or needing time to think it over. It was such a blessing to learn a better way than withdrawing! In Marriage Encounter we learned to write about our feelings. In Marriage Commitment we learned to use the knee-to-knee exercise to which Antony and Elsebeth referred.

It is a sign of real progress when the couple can get past the "silent" method and begin to communicate about the problem and its effects on each of them. They are then ready for the following steps.

1. *Time and setting are both important when a couple is working on an issue.* It is best to avoid times when either is tired and/or hungry. The setting should be private, without interruptions from people or the phone. It should be an agreed-upon time. While counseling, I found many couples with differing temperaments. One partner wants to settle the problem right now, and the other one wants to have time to figure it out and think it over before talking about it. It is so helpful if the one who needs time will say, "I need some time to think this through," or "I am feeling too emotional about this now. Can we talk about this in an hour?" (Or whatever time is needed.) Then make a definite appointment for the discussion. It is very important to follow through on this appointment, because problems have a tendency to get bigger rather than smaller when ignored.

2. *Sitting down knee to knee, while holding hands and expressing love for the mate, removes the concern that this discussion will be confrontational, and it demonstrates caring.* Making a statement at the outset, such as "I will not attack or blame you; I only want to share with you in 'I' statements something that is bothering me," further assures the other person that this is a safe exchange, and that there is no need to feel tension.

Antony and Elsebeth mentioned that they use "I" statements instead of "you" statements. For those of you who aren't familiar with these terms, here is an example of two possible ways to state a problem. Try to imagine what a difference it would make if you were the one on the receiving end of these two statements.

YOU STATEMENT: "You are always late, and you make me be late to everything." Another one would be "You make me so angry when you are always late."

I STATEMENT: "I really have a problem with lateness. I strive to be on time so as not to inconvenience other people. It does upset me; so can you help me to be on time?"

The main difference is that the speaker is taking responsibility for his/her own feelings instead of blaming or attacking the other person. Obviously, the other person doesn't mind being late and is not troubled by it so would not want to be blamed for the mate's feelings.

It's also wise to avoid the use of such words as "always," "never," and "all the time." They are too general and usually exaggerate the situation.

Good resolution comes when a couple works on the problem and doesn't attack each other's character.

It is amazing what a difference these strategies can make. It takes time to form new habits, but be patient with yourselves. We have found ourselves sometimes falling into old communication patterns. Then one of us will remember and say, "I'm sorry; I've slipped back into an old pattern. Let's start over again."

Here's another exercise that can be very useful when there's a deadlock. It utilizes some of the same methods mentioned earlier, such as using "I" statements.

Principle One: Listen carefully to each other and check out the meaning until you clearly understand from where the other person is coming. Use "I" messages when stating your case: "I just love that rock garden with its colorful flowers", "I get really turned off by that turquoise color on the exterior." No blaming or attacking.

Principle Two: Identify the needs of your mate. If you have listened carefully, this is not difficult to do. Check with your mate to see if you have identified those needs correctly.

Principle Three: Brainstorm by considering and listing *all* possible solutions.

Principle Four: Select the solution on which you can both agree and feel comfortable doing. Even if it takes a lot of dialoging, be patient. It's worth taking the time.

Let's look at the five most commonly used methods of dealing with conflict. Which one(s) do you use? Remember, the objective in friendships is to strengthen this relationship and to help each person meet his/her needs.

I mentioned that I used to *withdraw,* which is the worst of all the alternatives. It leaves the *goal* unachieved and sacrifices the *relationship*—two most important reasons for the friendship. The withdrawing person does not want to own the problem, the solution, or the relationship, and may be running away.

Then there are those for whom *winning* is very important. Winning achieves the goal, but at the sacrifice of the relationship. The winning mentality wants to own the solution to the problem, often leaving the other person feeling beaten and resentful. Not only does the winner want to win, he/she wants to win all the time. If you have this mentality, have you ever thought to ask yourself this question: "Who wants to be married to a loser?" That's what the other person becomes!

What about *yielding*? While yielding maintains the relationship and gives the appearance that all is well, the *sacrifice* of the goal is often a high price to pay and frequently results in quiet bitterness or increasing resentment. There may be times that yielding is appropriate and is done as a gift of love, but beware if the same person is the only one who always yields.

A good strategy is *compromise* that attempts to work out a solution by having all parties in the conflict give up something. If the process is done in a democratic fashion, everyone gains something (perhaps not the complete objective) and the relationship is strengthened. However, both may feel they have lost something.

The method we like the best is *creative solution*. This negotiation process is democratic in procedure and attempts to find the best solution for the objective and the relationship. It is characterized by direct and open communication, while brainstorming all possible options, then selecting the one that best meets the need. This results in real growth for the relationship, and no one is the loser. The following example illustrates how *creative solution* is different from *compromise*.

It is vacation time, and Bob wants to go mountain climbing, while Betty wants to spend time at the beach. A compromise might be to go visit relatives instead, with neither getting to do his/her favorite activity. A creative solution might be to find a vacation spot that has both mountains and the beach, and then do some of both together.

H. Norman Wright, a well-known author and speaker on the topic of good marital communication, made the statement that "when couples become sensitive to each other's needs and discuss these differences openly, adjustments are made and each partner achieves satisfaction."

And you know what? When this happens, it is *soooo* easy to kiss and make up!

Chapter 10

WHO GETS THE LAST WORD?

Peggy and Roger's Story

Concerning decision-making in marriage, you have probably heard people say that if there comes a time when the two spouses don't agree on some issue, that the husband, who is the head of the house, will need to make the final decision. That may be true in some marriages, but in our marriage of more than 50 years we have always been able to come to a decision that both of us find comfortable and can support.

We would like to share two examples of really heavy-duty decisions and the principles by which we arrived at these decisions, because we have found them to work so well, and they are too good to keep to ourselves. The first experience had to do with buying a house, and the second one had to do with whose career needed to receive precedence (a situation that arises often in two-career marriages).

Roger had accepted a position at Andrews University, and he was excited about this opportunity. This didn't pose a sacrifice for me, and I joyfully packed while envisioning an undergraduate and master's degree. We found a house to rent until we could sell ours. The owners wanted the house back when they returned from the mission field in six months, which we felt would pose no problem. But now the six months were coming to an end, and we hadn't found "our" house. God had blessed the sale of our home in Maryland (that promise in Malachi has proved itself over and over), and we were ready to buy one in Berrien Springs.

It wasn't that there weren't houses on the market—there were many. We were looking at the eighteenth house, but none was quite right for both of us. I wanted to be near the university to minimize winter driving in Michigan. We both wanted a moderately priced house, as it's been our habit to avoid huge mortgages. Roger wanted a nice view and a yard with privacy yet with not too much lawn to mow. I wanted a house that was nicely appointed and not too out-of-date. (We had been living in some rental properties for four years that lacked aesthetic qualities.)

Finally we found a nearly-new house that was in beautiful condition, inside and outside, and the interior and exterior were beautifully decorated. It was ready to move into without having to spend time redecorating, and it appealed to my sense of style. But it seemed a bit too expensive, and there was a foundation problem.

One day we were visiting a friend who was recovering from hip surgery, and we were talking about our dilemma. She told us that her neighbors were going to place their house on the market in a few days, and we should look into that possibility. This we did. Roger thought this was the one for us. I felt it seemed a bit outdated (it was built in the 1960s) and worn. After all, this was my opportunity to go back to school, and I wanted to get started on my education, not spend my time fixing up an older house.

As we talked about our individual choices for "our" house, we could see that there were two major considerations, plus a number of lesser ones. For Roger location was the most important. He would say, "The three most important considerations are location, location, location. Once you buy the house, there is nothing one can do about the location." After all the years of living in shabby or worn houses, I was ready for something that expressed my personality. I wanted flowers and trees in the yard, clean carpeting without pet odors, and some up-to-date features.

After considering all possible options, this is how we arrived at a solution that we both agreed upon and appreciated. Roger asked me if this compromise would work: What if we purchased the turquoise house that our friend had recommended, and that he liked so well, with the rock garden and the beautiful view on the ravine? It was even within easy walking distance from the university. This would meet his need—even as far as not having a big lawn to mow.

But then to meet my needs he suggested this solution: *I could change the house any way I wanted.* Because it met the requirements of being near the university, the price was right, the house was well built, it was clean, and we could take our time remodeling, I happily agreed on the purchase of this house.

The first project was to repaint the house to a more neutral color to match the brick. The next few months were quite messy, with plaster dust, painting, rug laying, pulling out dark paneling, redoing the fireplace, installing new soffits, etc. One day Roger said, "I never knew a house could be changed in so many ways!"

And we are both happy with the choice we made. It was a very good one for both of us. We have spent many happy years in this house (21 at this writing). But now it is outdated again and in need of more change. Are you ready for this, Roger?

Here are some principles in decision-making that have been very helpful to us:

1. We prayed and asked God for guidance in making the decision.
2. We involved all in the process who would be affected by the decision.
3. We clarified our goals and values.
4. We looked at long-term and short-term results that would occur.
5. We looked at all possible alternatives.
6. We collected information and consulted those with more experience.
7. We allowed sufficient time for this process.
8. Then we prayerfully decided on the course that was best for both of us.

As was mentioned earlier, marriages in which both partners have career goals can run into a challenge when one partner has the opportunity for an occupational move that may not be advantageous to the profession of the other spouse.

We were living in the Chesapeake Conference (Maryland), where

Roger was very busy as the superintendent of education and director of youth ministries for the conference. Cheryl, our daughter, had just graduated from Highland View Academy. I had returned to school to resume the registered nurse program at the local community college and had plans to continue at Johns Hopkins School of Nursing.

The delay in my education had occurred because I had dropped out of the nursing program at Washington Missionary College (now Columbia Union College) some years before. Roger had completed his undergraduate degree one year before I was scheduled to finish, and we wanted to get married before he left for a teaching appointment. (Marriage was not permitted in the nursing program at that time.) Now, years later, with Cheryl going off to college, it seemed the perfect time for me to return to the academic world.

One day in August Roger came home and said that he had received a request to consider becoming the principal of Mount Vernon Academy in Ohio. The board chair had asked that we fly to Mount Vernon for an interview if we would seriously consider the offer. There were only a few weeks before the school year was to begin, and the current principal had just left for another position. He emphasized that the need was urgent!

We never made decisions without consulting each other, and we never went ahead with any plans until we both agreed upon them. So Roger asked the inevitable questions: Would I be willing to go look at the situation? Would I be willing to move there if it seemed like the Lord's leading?

This was where my struggle began in earnest. Roger had mentioned from time to time that he would someday like to be the principal of an academy. He had had some interesting experiences as a student in boarding school, as a teacher, and as a youth leader that would enable him to address some of the problems he had seen develop among our youth. So I knew this was an opportunity he had been hoping for. I also sensed that there was a serious need at Mount Vernon Academy, as it was too late in the year for them to call someone from another school.

Then there were my needs that weren't the same at all and caused me considerable dissonance. I really enjoyed the house in which we were living that was right across the highway from the conference office. We had actually lived there for five years, in contrast to previous two- and three-year stints as Roger moved up the career ladder. And then there was my career. I had worked as a part-time secretary and a full-time mom, but now I was ready to accomplish my childhood dream—to be a nurse. In order for my local school of nursing to accept me into its program I would have to repeat courses and to challenge courses so that my transcript would fit into its module. This had been accomplished, and now I had just three more classes to complete. I dreaded going through this transfer hassle again.

But what would God have me do? Cheryl was now ready to begin the nursing program at Southern Missionary College (now Southern Adventist University), so our move would not affect her. Roger and I prayed earnestly for guidance and decided to take a look at Mount Vernon and get more information, such as whether I could transfer into a program somewhere near the academy.

We went for the interview. There were both positive and negative considerations, and we prayed much for guidance. There was a great need for a principal. We found that there was one school of nursing that would accept at least some of my credits. I would have to challenge some of the classes that I had already completed, and even repeat a course or two because they had to be taken in residence at that university. After considering all the facts I felt that even though it would prolong the obtaining of my degree, I should encourage Roger. He wanted to give it a try if I was of the same mind. Part of the agreement was that he would go with me to find a nursing school that would accept me at this late date in the fall.

There were many challenges as a result of this move. Sometimes we wondered if we had made the right decision. As we look back, though, we realize that God had much to teach us, even though the learning experience was not easy. A friend of mine who lived in Mount Vernon said, "I wish you hadn't come, because this is such a difficult time for this school. They've had a succession of principals, none of whom have stayed more than a year or two. I don't want to see you go through that kind of experience."

She wasn't exaggerating! Besides other difficulties confronting me, I had to drive 45 miles each way over hilly country roads to the University of Ohio (Zanesville campus) for my classes. School had already begun by the time we were able to move. I wasn't able to become involved in the activities of the academy because of my heavy program of study and clinical requirements at the hospital in Zanesville.

But as always, God is so good. We moved into a beautiful year-old home that was nicer than the one we left. For traveling on the wintry roads at 4:00 a.m. so I could be to the hospital on time, I had a very reliable bright-orange Volkswagen with studded tires (they were still legal at that time and enabled me to negotiate the hills in ice storms). God enabled me to pass the challenge exams (the first exam was to provide care to a severely burned patient who required reverse isolation techniques). Roger managed to hang in for two years. I graduated, passed state boards with flying colors, and earned my registered nurse status.

What I really appreciated was that Roger never pressured me to accept the move or said, "I am the head of the house, and so I get the last word." Because I grew up in a male-dominated home, that would have been really difficult for me to accept. Even when the going was hard, neither one of us could say to the other, "Why did you bring us here?"

Some principles that have worked really well for us are those I've already mentioned, plus a few that didn't apply in this situation:

1. We carefully explore and understand the feelings that lie behind the convictions of each person involved.

2. We never make a decision that will affect our mate without working it out together.

3. We never impose a condition on our mate with which he/she does not feel comfortable.

4. We give priority to the one who will be the most affected by the decision.

5. We give priority to the one who is dealing with an ethical, moral, and/or spiritual value.

Even though I placed my educational needs on hold a number of times during Roger's career, God and Roger enabled me to finish my career with an M.A. and a Ph.D. in counseling without taking opportunities away from our daughter and my husband. I also found an extremely satisfying later life career as a licensed professional counselor. In this capacity I served more than 11 years at the Andrews University Counseling and Testing Center.

It's easy to see how this method of making decisions eliminates power struggles, because the needs of both are carefully considered, and both spouses make the decision together. The wife is considering the needs of her husband, and the husband is considering the needs of his wife. In this manner both are getting their needs met, not because they are grasping to meet their own needs or because they have more power, but because they are working to meet the needs of their mate.

Chapter 11

DON'T BREAK MY COOKIES!

Teri and Richard's Story

*A*best-loved poem of a generation or so ago was "The Fool's Prayer," by American poet Edward Rowland Sill. To get the full setting, we will quote all of this brief poem, but we are primarily interested in three stanzas (italicized).

> The royal feast was done; the king
> Sought some new sport to banish care,
> And to his jester cried: "Sir Fool,
> Kneel now, and make for us a prayer!"
>
> The jester doffed his cap and bells,
> And stood the mocking court before;

They could not see the bitter smile
Behind the painted grin he wore.

He bowed his head, and bent his knee
Upon the monarch's silken stool;
His pleading voice arose: "O Lord,
Be merciful to me, a fool!

"No pity, Lord, could change the heart
From red with wrong to white as wool;
The rod must heal the sin: but Lord,
Be merciful to me, a fool!

"'Tis not by guilt the onward sweep
Of truth and right, O Lord, we stay;
'Tis by our follies that so long
We hold the earth from heaven away.

"These clumsy feet, still in the mire,
  Go crushing blossoms without end;
  These hard, well-meaning hands we thrust
  Among the heartstrings of a friend.

"The ill-timed truth we might have kept,
  Who knows how sharp it pierced and stung?
  The word we had not sense to say,
  Who knows how grandly it had rung?

"Our faults no tenderness should ask,
  The chastening stripes must cleanse them all;
  But for our blunders, oh, in shame
  Before the eyes of heaven we fall.

"Earth bears no balsam for mistakes;
  Men crown the knave, and scourge the tool
  That did his will; but Thou, O Lord,

Be merciful to me, a fool!"

The room was hushed; in silence rose
The king, and sought his gardens cool,
And walked apart, and murmured low,
"Be merciful to me, a fool!"

"You Always Hurt the One You Love." A popular song of some years back expresses the same truth found in those three italicized stanzas. We don't deliberately set out to hurt our mates. Nevertheless, in the course of the daily grind we *do* injure each other—sometimes very much. It's those "clumsy feet" that "go crushing blossoms." It's those "hard hands" among the delicate "heartstrings." It's speaking the truth without love that pierces and stings. It's failing to speak the word of support and affirmation. Not our deliberate meanness (though some of us suffer from that, too), but our blunders tear into sensitive feelings. How often we need to bow our heads and implore: "God, be merciful to me, a fool."

Richard and Teri Rose learned what to do when one hurts another. They are a special couple. Richard has spent years as a Seventh-day Adventist minister, and Teri is a nurse with the Visiting Nurse Association, specializing in new moms and their babies. Their daughter, Delfina, is studying at Southern Adventist University; and their son, Ralph, is in high school. Listen to their story.

❖ ❖ ❖

TERI: When we were engaged, I remember thinking of the big step we were taking and the responsibility that it entailed. I wished there had been premarriage counseling to help prepare us for success in our lifetime commitment, but there wasn't any on our college campus. Instead, we read together *The Adventist Home,* by Ellen White. It covered many subjects we wouldn't have automatically thought of discussing. It was fun to share our ideas with the guidance that book brought.

RICHARD: Since then we've read many other books that helped us to build on what we found as we read and discussed *The Adventist Home* together. We also went through a variety of experiences that taught us lessons that helped us build our future marriage relationship. As the first

Christmas of our marriage approached, Teri and I were teaching at Hylandale Academy in Wisconsin. We were making so little money that when I got drafted into the Army a few months later, I got a raise.

There was no money for Christmas gifts, let alone for a tree or decorations. In the woods we were able to cut down a large Christmas tree that we dragged home through the snow. The branches were so full at the bottom that it held itself up without any base on it. The tree took up a big space in our sparsely furnished living room.

TERI: I was so excited about our first Christmas, and I had never imagined that we would have a tree so big it reached the ceiling! I made real cookies for tree ornaments.

RICHARD: A few days before Christmas, Teri asked me to move a dresser into the extra bedroom on a Saturday night. I didn't want to do it, but she kept after me.

TERI: It would just take a minute to move the dresser, and my younger brother, who was there, could help.

RICHARD: Finally I relented, but I was exasperated with Teri. I enlisted my brother-in-law, Gerald, to help me move the dresser. I chose to take it through the living room, much to my later regret. As we went through the living room, we brushed the dresser against the Christmas tree. Gerald wondered if we should stop, but I was impatient with Teri and just wanted to get the job done. As we pressed on by the tree, we jostled the branches so much that the cookies fell to the floor.

TERI: I heard a crash and went into the living room, where I saw the tree had fallen. No problem. I could just pick it up and right it again. But there, on the floor, was a pile of broken cookies. All my hard work was destroyed. I ran to the bedroom and flung myself over the bed, trying hard not to be heard crying.

RICHARD: When I came back into the living room after moving the dresser, I knew that something was seriously wrong. I went into the bedroom, and there was Teri, lying on the bed, crying very hard. I sat down beside her and asked her what was the matter. She was crying so hard she couldn't say anything at first.

TERI: Between sobs I finally choked out, "You . . . you . . . you broke . . . my . . . cookies!"

RICHARD: When Teri told me why she was crying, I immediately felt remorse. I told her we could make more cookies, and other soothing things, but nothing I said seemed to comfort her.

TERI: Richard patted me and said he was sorry. He seemed to really care and, of course, I forgave him. I never had time to make more cookies.

RICHARD: I think the fact that Teri wasn't able to make any more cookies reinforced for me an important lesson from that Christmas experience. After acting impulsively, it is not always possible to make everything completely right in a marriage. Better to give some thought first. But the experience also proved to have positive lessons for our marriage as well.

TERI: Today, 30 short years later, we don't agree on every detail as to why or how the "cookie tragedy" happened, or why Richard was peeved about moving the dresser. Those details are forgiven and forgotten. The important thing is that we have been using this experience to better communicate an understanding of each other's hopes and dreams.

Whenever we come to a situation that one of us cares a lot about, we will just say, "Don't break my cookies." That is a gentle reminder that conveys a great deal of experience and emotion and helps us recognize when there is a need not to press too hard or to be more supportive. "Don't break my cookies" is a way of speaking our own language. We used it often in the early years of our marriage. Our relationship eventually grew past the point of needing to employ that phrase very often.

Christmas trees and cookies no longer seem so important. I learned that *things* in life are not nearly as valuable as our relationship. Another device that we used to communicate in the early years of our marriage was a mascot—a little yellow, squeaky, rubber duck.

RICHARD: After Teri told me about losing a pet duck she loved, I went out and bought her a rubber duck for a present.

TERI: The words of the then-popular song "Rubber Ducky," expressed care and fondness. Besides fun and play, it was easy to project our thoughts and feelings through the rubber duck. Eventually we communicated better and didn't have to tell each other what the "rubber duck" wanted or felt.

RICHARD: Our living room is our worship room. Today we read the Bible and other Christian books to the family. We have chosen not to have a television so we can control what is seen and heard inside our home. All members of the family join together for devotions and prayer. When the children were younger, we would often read a continued story. The entire family looks forward to this time together. If one of us is gone, the other will lead out.

◆ ◆ ◆

Since we have such great potential to "hurt the one we love," it will pay to stop and think before we speak or act. Rather than blundering our way through, pause and consider the effect of our words and actions. It is better to maintain a loving relationship than to try to repair a damaged one. In the words of Will Carleton's poem:

Boys flying kites haul in their white-winged birds;
You can't do that when you're flying words.
"Careful with fire," is good advice we know;
"Careful with words" is ten times doubly so.
Thoughts unexpressed may sometimes fall back dead,
But God Himself can't kill them when they're said.

But let's admit it—we're imperfect humans. In spite of our best intentions, we will, at times, wound the one we love. Here too, Richard and Teri have some good advice for us: "Admit we are wrong; say we are sorry; ask for forgiveness; comfort the sorrowing one. If we have been on the wronged end of the equation, freely forgive and don't keep bringing it up in the future."

To keep your marriage brimming,
With love in the loving cup,
Whenever you're wrong, admit it;
Whenever you're right, shut up!
                              —Ogden Nash*

Finally, notice the emphasis that Richard and Teri give to family worship. The presence of Jesus in the home and in the heart is a healing balm and a great preventive against thoughtless words and acts that fracture relationships. Walking with Jesus will help us keep from breaking those cookies.

---

*Ogden Nash, "A Word to Husbands," in *I Wouldn't Have Missed It: Selected Poems of Ogden Nash* (Little, Brown and Company, 1975), p. 334.

Chapter 12

BALANCING THE LOVE BANK

Dorothy and Bruce's Story

Most of us have checking accounts. You know how that works. You can draw money out and write checks on the account as long as you keep depositing enough funds to maintain a positive balance. If you take out more than you put in, your check is going to bounce. You'll get the dread notice from your bank: insufficient funds.

Marriage is a lot like a checking account. Every negative interaction depletes to some extent your love bank. Every way that husbands and wives support each other, encourage each other, and demonstrate love to each other puts more deposits in that bank. If you wish to have a happy, successful marriage, you'd better make more deposits than withdrawals. It's as simple as that.

We remember Bruce and Dorothy Hayward from the time they came to Andrews University as students. Dorothy excelled in the community counseling program, and Bruce was a diligent seminary student. After graduation they both worked in Canada (their home) for a time, and then returned to work in the Berrien Springs Village Seventh-day Adventist Church, where Bruce serves as one of the pastors. Dorothy established and manages the WellSpring Family Life and Counseling Ministry. They share their story.

❖ ❖ ❖

BRUCE: It's been 30 years since we started our life together. When we got married, we thought we could never love each other more, only longer. But in every relationship there are ups and downs, and ours is no exception. The concept of the love bank, which is talked about by several different authors, is an apt description of what has taken place in our relationship. We've discovered that when the withdrawals take place, we just have to work harder to increase the deposits.

Our first year was spent in Korea as student missionaries. Nearly losing Dorothy to dysentery less than a month after our marriage helped me see that one could not take life for granted. That year was a real growth experience. Adjusting to marriage while living in a house with three other couples, all married less than three months, teaching English seven hours a day, living in a culture that is vastly different from our own, had a real maturing influence on us.

We married before we finished college, and planned to return to school after our year in Korea. However, the need to earn money for tuition postponed that. On account of a variety of circumstances, we ended up entering the work force and starting our family. God gave us our first precious baby in 1975, and just five weeks after she was born we found our whole family living in a truck temporarily as we traveled throughout western Canada on the Adventist Book Center bookmobile.

There were many opportunities to grow in Christian graces while we lived in tight quarters with a tiny one who consumed much of our time and energy, sandwiched between demanding book sales and long hours of travel through those mountain passes and endless prairie highways. We recall fondly the happy memories that we built together in those days, but we also recognize that the growth in our relationship was in spite of ourselves, because we were two strong personalities.

During the first year of Darla's life she had a full-time mom and dad, food that was ever ready (Dorothy nursed her), and a daddy who proudly introduced her to the many people who came to the bookmobile. This served to make her a social and outgoing baby, and that has been a strong point in her personality ever since. It was a rich bonding period for all of us.

Much as we loved our time together, we had hard decisions to make, as travel became impossible with a toddler who would walk along and pull price stickers off the books or become disgruntled with long hours of riding. Schedules didn't allow us to stop and stretch or play at a park nearly long enough for our precious Darla. God's grace was evident in those experiences, however, because of the large deposits made in our family love banks for each other. With our second child, Dora, on the way, we decided it was time for Mom to stay home.

As with most young families living on one income, finances were a huge trial, along with other challenges that surfaced. Job demands were high, and it seemed the work was never done. There were 14- to 16-hour days when Daddy was in town, then he was often gone out of town on business trips for several days or weeks at a time. Dorothy's role as a married-single mom, home full-time with two little ones and much of the time with no vehicle, caused hours of questioning. She had hopes and dreams for herself, and soiled diapers, crying babies, piles of dirty dishes, and loads of laundry were not part of her personal fulfillment dream, even though raising the children had its own special rewards. She loved people and social interaction, so being stuck with kids and limited social outlets resulted in high levels of inner turmoil and huge withdrawals from her love bank for the marriage relationship.

My workaholism that consumed my life left little time for marriage development and partnership parenting. Sometimes well-intended church and missionary activities served to undermine the meaningfulness of the few hours we were able to spend together, because of physical fatigue, mental distractions, and constant preoccupation with our varied and separate lives. We can't remember that the marriage commitment was ever seriously questioned, but the responsibilities we each carried and our personal spiritual journey through those years certainly impacted how we dealt with one another during the rougher years in our marriage relationship.

DOROTHY: There were years of church planting, home schooling, running the school lunch program, being a homeroom mom, and later, substitute teaching. All this filled my life while Bruce committed more than full time to the demanding ministry at the Adventist Book Center. During those years we moved frequently and built treasured memories with extended family and friends.

The devil has many ways of planting distractions in our lives—female work colleagues with inappropriate intentions, the premature termination of a pregnancy (it was our boy), computers, and financial demands on many sides. How do the members of a young family survive on one denominational salary, live in conference-provided housing, and feel as though they can get ahead or save toward the future? It takes faith and management skills beyond what came naturally for us.

After 14 years of marriage that included 10 years of parenting, God arranged in our lives a bigger challenge—a return to school for higher education, along with the family, financial, and academic dilemmas that come with it. If we had thought it was hard to keep the love bank accounts in order before, it became nearly overwhelming now. During those eight years we attended Canadian Union College, interned in a pastorate, and then both earned master's degrees at Andrews University.

I had come from a large family and, like many, was threatened with identity confusion and low self-worth. God blessed me with a man who tirelessly affirmed me, believed in me, has succeeded to help me stabilize my self-confidence with God, and given me confidence as I have pursued my career in counseling psychology.

BRUCE: Dorothy's family is three times as large as mine. There were five years between my older sister and me, and another five years between my younger brother and me. By the time I became a teenager my older brother was already gone from home. While my family was close, because of the age spread there were times that I felt as if I was growing up alone.

I learned at a very early age to be a workaholic. At age 12 I began riding my bike five miles every summer day to work on a farm that was owned by family friends. For nine summers I worked, putting in 16- to 18-hour days five and a half days a week. That work ethic carried into my adult life and still has an impact on my ability to take time for my family.

Most marriages are put to the test when children and parenting issues become intense. We both loved and were committed to our children; however, when teenage rebellious independence hit our family, we literally had to cling to the Lord and to each other. The love-bank accounts for all four of our nuclear family members were often depleted by misunderstandings, disappointed dreams, and individual choices that for a time turned family harmony into emotional and relational chaos.

Today both of our daughters are married, and three beautiful and delightful granddaughters continue to unfold the life cycle. Through sickness and health, prosperity and adversity, there continues to be loss of focus from time to time, but, praise God, our marital commitment deepens, and we still feel that we can't possibly love each other deeper—just longer. And we pray that through eternity that love will become enriched and magnified in the presence of our Maker, Redeemer, and heavenly Father.

The Haywards have experienced enough strains and frustrations to fracture some marriages. Yet they are survivors, still in love. They have managed to overcome the obstacles and build a satisfying relationship. How did they do it? They were intentional about making deposits in their love bank. They did things that cemented their marriage and affirmed their love. They had enough in that bank that they could afford the inevitable withdrawals. That's what all of us need to do. We can't avoid problems, but we can build a relationship strong enough to handle them.

Chapter 13

BLENDING TWO FAMILIES— HIS AND HERS

Bonnie and George's Story

eorge and Bonnie Knight met at Andrews University, where George is a professor of church history at the Theological Seminary, a prolific writer with many published works, and an international presenter. Bonnie was working as a secretary in the Institute of Hispanic Studies at the time they met. Since their marriage she has retired from that position so she can travel with George and be a full-time homemaker. How have they succeeded in making a viable blended family? Here is the story in their own words.

❖ ❖ ❖

GEORGE: Second marriages aren't always easy, especially when children are involved. Especially when the children are teenagers. And especially when *both* partners have children.

The two of us were absolutely convinced that we were for each other, but we were equally committed to the fact that our relationship had to be one that all of our children and grandchildren would be able to joyfully accept and find to be a personal blessing. Both of us were committed parents who did not want to put our wishes above the health of our respective families.

Those families, for better or worse, were quite different. Bonnie's children had been born and raised in Spain, while mine had never been outside of North America. And then there was the matter of the age differences of our children. At the time we started seeing each other, hers were 14 and 11, while mine were 29 and 28. Beyond that, I also had grandchildren, who were 11 and 8. Thus, if we were to marry, we would face the rather interesting prospect of our youngest child being the same age as our oldest grandchild. Hardly the typical normal family!

The two of us aren't that far apart in age. I'm 10 years older, but had my children while I was in my early 20s. Bonnie had hers in her late 20s and early 30s. This explains the larger age differential of the children in our rather atypical family. The challenge we faced was one of blending two quite different families. How to go about the task became one of our first considerations as we discussed a more serious relationship.

One of our first decisions set the agenda for our courtship. Early on we agreed that we would call off our personal plans if any one of our four children did not feel comfortable with the idea of a possible marriage. Of course, we never told the children of that pact. In fact, we never provided them with the slightest hint that they had any power over the relationship. But in our minds we wanted the best for both them and our possible future marriage. We knew that a marriage couldn't reach its full potential unless each of the children was rejoicing in the relationship.

Well, you may be thinking, how did we go about our relationship? Once our goals and priorities were clear, we knew exactly what we had to do. We had to make each child feel comfortable in our relationship. As a result, our families became the focal point of our courtship. Time together often meant an evening of entertainment at Bonnie's house with her two children, the four of us playing table games as we got to know each other better. At other times it meant going to the beach, going bowling, or taking the kids out for dinner and ice cream.

Then there was the challenge of George's two children, who both had been married for some years. Sabbath dinners, game nights, and family camping times became central in bringing the two families together. In the process of putting our children first, none of them came to fear that he or she was losing a parent to some stranger. To the contrary, all of them came to see that they were gaining a parent.

That is just what we had hoped for. As the children (grown and otherwise) became comfortable with the new relationship(s), we began to move toward a marriage about which everyone was excited.

The marriage ceremony itself was also a combined family affair. All the children and grandchildren had a major part in the wedding, and the entire united family closed the service with a circle of prayer on the platform. That prayer circle symbolized the unity that we had worked so hard to achieve.

As you can see, we didn't really have much of a dating experience before we were married. The real dating started after we were wife and husband. Then at last we found more time to be alone. But that did not prove to be a hardship on the children. By that time they knew that Mom and Dad needed some special time together.

In many ways there were no big shocks after the marriage. The two families had already been blending, and our marriage was merely a continuation of those things with which they were already comfortable.

Some people may not think that starting a marriage with a 12- and a 15-year-old in the house is a formula for success, but in our case it couldn't have worked out more smoothly. Why? Because the children, all of them, were never outside the relationship. We had consciously chosen to put them at the center from the beginning. That choice paid big dividends.

BONNIE: We have now been married seven years. How, you may be thinking, has this affected our blending? The blending has merely gotten better and better. We still camp together from time to time, play games, and enjoy one another. One of the high points was the fourth summer of our marriage when nearly all of the combined family spent two weeks together in a shared condo in Hawaii. That two weeks brought about a bonding that was very special. By that time the age differences between our younger children and the grandchildren made less of a difference than they had earlier, and deeper common interests were discovered as we intensely lived and played together.

We look back at our marriage and our united family and praise God that He led us to put Him and our families at the center of our relationship rather than merely our desires and pleasures. Sure, it would have been nice to be able to spend more personal time together early on. We knew that. But our real concern was with the long run rather than the short. Having a blended family has made it much easier to have a blended marriage.

Before closing our story, we should note that everything has not gone perfectly in our united family. Early in the marriage the inevitable tensions between my children and your children developed between the two of us. On the other hand, even though such episodes created a bit of tension from time to time, they were not overly problematic because both of us had already demonstrated that we loved the other's children and had been willing to sacrifice for them. Then again, each of the children knew that the new parent genuinely and deeply cared about him/her. That opened up channels of communication between parents and their new children that would not have been possible had the children not been central from the beginning. In line with those open channels of communication we chose not to intercede when any problem arose between our spouse and his or her new stepchild. Rather, the two parties talked, face to face. In that way walls were not built up, and the blending could proceed even in troublesome times. Thus, we discovered that even potential disasters could be turned into blessings if we were willing to put some effort into the foundation we had so carefully chosen to lay in our dating experience.

GEORGE: All we can say after seven years is Praise God for all His blessings in our blended family, including the addition of a 3-year-old grandson. We've enjoyed the blending so far and, given the scattered ages of our children and grandchildren, we look forward to a constant stream of more grandchildren and great-grandchildren in the years to come.

❖　❖　❖

REBUILDING ONE'S LIFE AND FAMILY AFTER A DIVORCE

This is the challenge that one in four Adventists face (Monte and

Norma Sahlin, *A New Generation of Adventist Families* [Center for Creative Ministry, 1997], p. 8). This ideally begins with divorce counseling for parent and child and a period of grief and healing (some professionals recommend at least two years). And then the work can begin on rebuilding.

Thus, George and Bonnie have opened a private window and shared with all of us how they prayerfully and intentionally put together their two families into one Christ-centered family that makes great effort to help each member feel important and loved. They put the needs of their children above their own because they wanted to do all they could to mitigate the trauma the children had already experienced.

Divorce impacts all family members, especially the children, who are the innocent victims. Judith Wallerstein chronicled these lasting effects in her 25-year landmark study of divorced families, *The Unexpected Legacy of Divorce* (2000). Children of divorce need to know they are important and that their parents will be there for them. The children in this family have been made a priority and given a sense of security that results from following an intentional plan.

Chapter 14

INSTANT MOTHERHOOD IN A PACKAGE-DEAL MARRIAGE

Millie and John's/Selma and Orlando's Stories

*L*et's suppose that you are a mature single woman who has never had any children of your own. You've seen other couples sharing life together, and you've wondered if there might be somebody who was right for you. Then you meet him. He is attractive and has many fine personal qualities. You are falling for him. One problem! He has children from his former marriage—even *teenagers*. You ask yourself: "Am I up to this?" Can I handle instant motherhood?

We have two submissions from couples John and Millie Youngberg and Orlando and Selma Mastrapa, who have achieved happy relationships despite the tragic losses that both husbands experienced. In both cases their first wives and the mothers of their children died from the dreadful disease of cancer. God wept with them as they suffered through the loneliness and disruption of their lives. Because of the blessed hope in the resurrection and with the faith that only God can provide, they determined to make as normal a family life as possible for their children and themselves. They have shared with their readers their personal journey in the expectation that their stories can be an encouragement to others going through a similar experience.

The first story is by the Youngbergs, the second by the Mastrapas. Rather than writing the stories as one voice, both couples have chosen to give their personal perspectives on how they were able to rebuild their families. Isaiah 61:3 uses the words "to appoint unto them that mourn in Zion, to give unto them beauty for ashes, the oil of joy for mourning, the garment of praise for the spirit of heaviness," that He might be glorified.

Since their marriage John and Millie have worked tirelessly in family life education. They founded the Marriage Commitment seminars and have conducted scores of seminars all over the world, as well as training other facilitators. They also founded and conducted Family Life International for 25 years. Both are retired professors from Andrews University, John in the family life area, and Millie as a reading specialist.

JOHN: When Bonnie, my first wife, died in March 1971, our family was shattered. She had been anointed twice. After five months of illness with a brain tumor, the pressure had been building. The children, John, Jr., and Wes (ages 12 and 10)—especially Wes—were having behavioral problems at school and were almost climbing the wall.

I went on a long walk one Sabbath afternoon down Pathfinder Hill in Berrien Springs. With the Lord I shared how heavy the pressure had become and my concern about being able to endure. My faith was renewed, and when I went back to the hospital where Bonnie lay in a coma, I was so sure she would be healed that I took along clothes for her so I could bring her home. But such was not to be. The next Wednesday she died.

The Ruth Murdoch Elementary School, where the children attended, pitched in, and the parents gave us a purse of more than $200. The Pioneer Memorial church, my fellow teachers at Andrews University, the community, and loved ones were marvelously supportive, and I can't tell you how much it all meant to me. As an adult with somewhat mature faith, I didn't feel that I had to understand the whys of our family tragedy. I could leave that in the hands of God, knowing that some day the answer would be plain. But for the children, it was a different scenario. God had failed them. On the tombstone in Rose Hill Cemetery our hope was recorded in granite. It pictures four interconnected links of a chain, and the second link is broken. Then there is recorded the promise as found in *The Desire of Ages:* "There will be a relinking of the family chain" (p. 632).

But life must go on. In life's game an important player may fall on the field, there may be a short timeout, but the game goes relentlessly on. Some months later Millie came into my life as a meaningful friend. She had met Bonnie once for about 30 seconds when we were returning a cassette player we had borrowed so as to tape *Your Story Hour* programs to take to our Bolivian mission field. Millie says if she had known what a vital part Bonnie was to play in the rest of her life, she would have protracted that momentary encounter.

I had inquired around for a class in speed note taking, and an Andrews staff member said that such a course was not taught at Andrews, but Millie Urbish taught a good course in speed reading. Thinking this would be ideal for my future doctoral studies, I showed up in Millie's dynamic reading class. The class had only three students. A friendship evolved between student and teacher, and I learned to read between the lines! That's what I call dynamic reading!

My loving, conservative mother frowned upon remarriage less than one year after the death of a spouse. But for such mundane considerations as saving considerable money on income tax deductions before the new year and the convenience of vacation dates (Millie taught at Andrews, and I was taking doctoral class work at Western Michigan University, and the two schools had different calendars), we married on December 21. Our pastor had another wedding the same day for a hippie couple, who had chosen the date because it was a propitious day—the winter solstice. But whatever the merits of such astrology, that date has proven to be a very propitious day for us and, by extension, to our family and to our ministry for families around the world.

It isn't easy to become the mother/stepmother of two lively boys. Bonnie had left an imprint that was almost bigger than life. She had invested her very life into her sons. The picture is still clear in my mind after 30 years of coming home from a night committee meeting at our college in Bolivia and finding my little flock all in one bed, sound asleep with the *My Bible Story* books strewn around the bed from story time. How could another fill those shoes?

Although the children had voted for Millie (they had a vote but not a veto), I should have been more sensitive to some of their perceptions. We had a lovely alpaca shawl from Bolivia that had been Bonnie's, and I gave it as a gift to Millie. Strangely, it disappeared a few days later, and look where we might, it could not be found. Many months later, when doing repair work above the ceiling tiles in son John's basement room, I found the missing shawl. In the minds of the boys, such a precious garment was not to be handed on to Bonnie's successor.

MILLIE: A mother is irreplaceable, but I still consider John, Jr., and Wes to be my boys, although I did not bear them. But adapting to the new home situation was not easy for them or for me—trying to be a good wife, mother, and a good daughter-in-law. (Grandma Youngberg lived in our basement apartment, and, to her credit, I must say that she never interfered and always, saint that she was, was supportive.)

Teaching full-time, finishing a house, and cooking meals for five instead of one was very stressful, and was too much. I began to get sick and had Ménière's attacks of dizziness. We had to do some home reorganizing. Each son had a To Do card of duties to be performed when he arrived home from school. At first the tasks were simple, i.e., dust the stereo, pull weeds for 10 minutes, etc., but soon the list grew longer, to the point that the boys were making a real difference in home routines.

Little by little our relationship grew, although interspersed with family crises. Husband John and I had minimal difficulties in adapting to marriage. But with the sons it was something else. We camped out or hiked in almost any park you could name in southwest and not-so-southwest Michigan. We canoed; we did lots of things as a family. Still, it was hard.

Once I asked John, "Will the boys ever love me?" to which he replied, "They will love and accept you by the time they reach 35." Well, praise God, they beat that by quite a few years. It is so wonderful to get on the phone with Wes at his mission appointment as a doctor of preventive care at the Guam Clinic and have him say with all naturalness, "I love you, Mom!" And the same with son John. He will say, "I love you," even if I forget. At the time of this writing Wes is 42 and John, Jr., is 43. John is principal of Guam Adventist Academy. We are proud grandparents of five! Want to see our pictures?

And marriage? It has grown sweeter as the years have gone by. At the altar we prayed our vows and promised to enhance and help each other to be all that we could be. That's what has been happening to us. God isn't through with us yet. We are still growing. The goal is in sight, and, hand in hand, we journey onward until heaven shall be our home.

JOHN: And Millie hasn't been just a pinch hitter or a substitute player. She has been a superstar in her own right!

❖ ❖ ❖

John and Millie have written many books about family life. Through the years they have practiced what they preached, as is evident by the solidarity of their family. This would be a good place to add to what they have already told us with some principles from Elizabeth Einstein's "How to Adjust to a 'Package' Deal Marriage" in her book *The Stepfamily: Living, Loving, and Learning* (MacMillan).

1. *Determine your own identity.* Stepfamilies are not the same as their biological counterparts.

2. *Be realistic.* You can't make stepfamilies into "natural" families, and it's best not to try.

3. *Expect conflicting emotions.* Don't raise your expectations of your feelings toward your stepchildren too high. Concentrate on your behavior and actions.

4. *Stick together.* Successful stepparents seem to have one thing in common—they recognize the necessity of working together as a couple, even though they don't agree on everything.

5. *Take a Christian perspective, rather than "What's in it for me?"* The goal becomes that of providing the children—his, hers, or ours—with a meaningful sense of a God-centered family.

❖ ❖ ❖

We first met Orlando Mastrapa and Selma Chaij at Andrews University long before they married. It was exciting to see their friendship develop into a permanent commitment. Selma, a clinical psychologist and an educator, was Peggy's professor. Orlando was a professor in the Modern Language Department.

ORLANDO: I was a widower at age 46, with three teenagers, and the thought of remarriage was overwhelming. Many prayers and meditations were part of my daily routine. God would have to help me find the best woman for my situation.

Since I worked on a university campus, most of the women I met were too young for me. After several years of being single, God showed me whom He had prepared for me. She was right there, in the church I attended every Sabbath!

Selma played the piano for worship services, we were colleagues at the university, and we had a similar culture and background. I considered those factors as very important for a successful marriage. Besides being attractive, she was a committed Christian and a lovely person.

Some time after we married, my second son decided to change careers. He didn't have enough resources to continue studying and paying household expenses. He needed help, and Selma immediately told him to come and live with us. Several months later another crisis occurred in the family. My oldest daughter was devastated when her husband asked for a divorce. Selma again invited her to move in with us.

My son finished his new career in a year and immediately found a satisfying job and an apartment that he could share with a roommate. However, he continues to maintain the warm and close relationship with Selma that developed from the unconditional acceptance and encouragement that he received during difficult times.

My daughter recovered from the shock of betrayal by her husband. Her healing from divorce was greatly facilitated by the supportive environment at home and because she did not have to go through it alone. Two years later she married a positive, committed, Christian man, and they have rediscovered the joy and depth of shared love.

For me it is wonderful to have a wife who cares and affirms my children and me. For her understanding, her commitment to God, her patience with me, and so many other beautiful attributes, I love her!

SELMA: It was not easy to trust again after the severity of pain I experienced from my divorce. After 12 years alone I had accepted the idea that I would be alone for the rest of my life. My prayer was that the Lord would lead me in all my ways and deliver me from any more destructive relationships. It was therefore an unexpected pleasure to discover that perhaps I might be able to feel love and affection again.

My first reaction toward Orlando was to push him away. However, as I was about to utter a flip and rejecting comment to him, I felt a voice within me saying, "No, this man has been hurt enough. Stay open to him."

As I became better acquainted with him, I admired his thoughtfulness with his aging and terminally ill parents. I had also heard how supportive he had been to his wife during her final illness. His determination to keep his family together had made him work extra hard to be a constant part of his children's lives. And he succeeded. He taught me how to relate to all children with his easy and warm charisma. As a career woman I had not realized how engrossed I had become in the adult world of work. He taught me how to play and enjoy simple relationships.

After our marriage we moved to a different state and a different career. It was difficult for me to become an immediate part of a very tightly knit family. However, I determined to wait silently and learn for as long as it should take to do so. After the first three years of marriage, I finally felt accepted by all my stepchildren. I was also blessed with two beautiful granddaughters. My granddaughters have taught me the most about what it takes to give and receive love.

Early in our marriage my husband realized that even though he enjoyed hard physical labor, I did not have the stamina for it. We both have a deep appreciation for aesthetics and a beautiful environment. He enjoys working in the yard and creating a beautiful landscape, but I just enjoy watching the results. I love a clean and neat home, but he took it upon himself to do the vacuuming and heavy labor. He never complains that he does all the hard work, and he knows how much I appreciate it.

I was first attracted to my husband because of his good looks, and I still enjoy his pulchritude. However, it is his kindness and his respect for me and for others that has deepened my love and admiration of him as a man and as a husband. It is a joy to see how true love brings out the best in the other person.

◆　◆　◆

We would like to reinforce the principles that Orlando and Selma used in rebuilding their family with the following information:

Knowing how to be a good stepparent is not something for which most persons have prepared. Fortunately, there are stepparents who have learned by experience and research and have written about what they have learned so others could benefit. Barbara L. Dowling wrote "Welcome to the Step Family" in the *Adventist Review* (Nov. 9, 1989). It is evident that Orlando and Selma incorporated these principles into their marriage. Dowling called these 11 principles "The Learning Curve for Stepparents."

1. Learn to place your spouse and your marriage first.

2. Learn empathy for your spouse's concerns.

3. Learn to accept your relationship with your stepchildren at whatever level it exists.

4. Learn to listen to each family member. Unless you have serious reasons to doubt, trust that what you are hearing is the truth.

5. Learn to concentrate on praising good behavior instead of criticizing bad behavior.

6. Learn to let go of your way and compromise.

7. Learn not to keep score.

8. Learn to focus on the desired outcome rather than the barriers to achieving it.

9. Learn to forgo asking for details about your spouse's former marriage. Build new memories.

10. Learn to bury your pride and be the first to love.

11. Learn to rely on the Lord continually. Recognize that you can't always fix your problems, so turn them over to God.

Chapter 15

LOVE GLUE

Jill and Allan's Story

*I*t would be difficult to overestimate the importance of the role of sex in a happy and successful marriage. While the actual act of sex occupies only a minor portion of married couples' time together, the sexual relationship is foundational to marriage.

This fact is revealed at the very beginning of Biblical history. Six times in the first chapter of Genesis God pronounces His creation to be "good." Yet after creating the man, placing him in the Edenic garden, and permitting him to name the animals, God finds something to be "not good." In the sinless perfection of Eden, whatever could not be good? "It is not good that the man should be alone" (Genesis 2:18).

So God creates Eve out of a part of Adam's body to show the close physical connection that was to be between them. Then He sets out the formula for marriage in one short verse: "A man will leave his father and mother and be united to his wife, and they will become one flesh" (Genesis 2:24, NIV). This is the most profound and basic description of marriage to be found in sacred Scripture. Both Jesus and Paul quote it in the New Testament when they are trying to explain the sacredness of marriage. While the "one flesh" focuses on the physical aspects of the husband-wife relationship, it also stands as a symbol of the spiritual, psychological, and social oneness that God intended for the married couple.

Whenever the Bible discusses sexuality in the context of the marriage relationship, it always emphasizes its goodness and importance. A few samples from the NIV must suffice:

"May your fountain be blessed, and may you rejoice in the wife of your youth. A loving doe, a graceful deer—may her breasts satisfy you always, may you ever be captivated by her love" (Proverbs 5:18, 19).

"Let my lover come into his garden and taste its choice fruits" (Song of Solomon 4:16).

"The wife's body does not belong to her alone but also to her husband. In the same way, the husbands body does not belong to him alone but also to his wife" (1 Corinthians 7:4).

"Marriage should be honored by all, and the marriage bed kept pure" (Hebrews 13:4).

The essential place of sexuality in the marriage relationship has been recognized in the laws of the land. A couple may have a legal wedding ceremony and a marriage license, but if they never follow with sexual relationships, the marriage is said to be not "consummated" and could be legally annulled.

Now, married couples who aren't able to have normal relationships because of medical reasons or advancing age may still have a tender and loving marriage, but this is not the original divine plan. The usual formula goes something like this: Married couples who have a satisfying and intimate sexual relationship have a happy and successful marriage. Those who have an unsatisfactory and unfulfilling sexual experience do not have a close relationship otherwise, and are not tasting all the possibilities of marital joy. We have formulated a hypothesis about this. We propose that when you see a longtime married couple walking hand in hand, with their arms around each other, or displaying affection in other ways, they are likely to be still sexually attracted to each other.

However, when we talk about sex we mean more than the mere act of coitus. Sexuality is far broader than that. It goes to the very root of our human existence and involves everything that defines us as "male" and "female." Walter Trobisch, a pastor and counselor, once wrote: " 'To become one flesh' means much more than just the physical union. It means that two persons share everything they have, not only their bodies, not only their material possessions, but also their thinking and their feeling, their joy and their suffering, their hopes and their fears, their successes and their failures. 'To become one flesh' means that two persons become completely one with body, soul, and spirit and yet there remain two different persons" (*I Married You,* [Harper & Row, 1971], p. 18).

This "one flesh" experience is the attraction that men feel for women and women feel for men that they do not experience with someone from their own gender. It includes the kisses and hugs that they exchange first thing in the morning, last thing at night, and whenever one of the couple leaves the home or returns to it. It may encompass embraces, fondling, and gentle pats on the backside. It is she sitting on his lap while they watch television. It involves long walks in the woods, hand in hand, tender words whispered in the ear, winks across a crowded room, and showering together. It exults in the simple joys of physical closeness. It is the pain of being separated and the thrill of coming back together. None of these things would exist if we were not sexual beings. Sex is the "love glue" that binds husband and wife together.

Now the bad part! While sex is ideally the bond of unity, it is also often a cause for conflict, unhappiness, and distancing. Couples may find themselves divided over such issues as frequency, appropriate methods, timing, place, and feelings of being used. How can something created to be the source of unity turn into something that divides and ruptures marital oneness? Further, how can married couples whose sex life is less than ideal turn it around and find once again the intimacy and oneness that the Creator intended? How can we go from the bad to the beautiful? That is really the subject of this chapter. That is the story we wish to share.

Let's face it—most people are hesitant to talk or write about a subject as sensitive as their personal sexual journey. But we thought right away about our friends Allan and Jill Kennedy, who have been long involved in

Marriage Encounter and other marriage enhancement programs. Because they had shared so openly about their sexual struggles in their marvelous book *Longing to Be Loved* (Pacific Press, 1997), we dared to ask them to tell their story here as an encouragement to other struggling couples. They graciously agreed.

◆ ◆ ◆

NOT TONIGHT, DEAR

ALLAN: Sexuality reveals much about who we really are. The "shoulds" and "shouldn'ts" of our life commandments shape us more in the area of sexuality than in any other; primarily because sexuality is an area that is seldom discussed and is many times secretive. If it is discussed, it is usually with a sense of uneasiness or embarrassment. I share my story with the hope that this can be used to bring encouragement to other fellow travelers.

Growing up on a farm with the opportunity to observe the birth of animals gave me some sense of how life began. But my sexual development, in many ways, was typical of numerous others. My earliest memory of personal sexuality was of a neighbor boy teaching me about masturbation. I remember the shame and embarrassment I felt. Only looking back, with the benefit of a lot of study, do I realize the far-reaching impact of that event. Today's backward view helps me to understand that I was set up by that event for much of my acting out—the push toward girlie magazines, the physical dimension of many of my relationships, and my rebellious spirit, all of which I brought with me as I entered marriage.

Typically, I discussed none of this prior to marriage with Jill. Probably, for one thing, I was unaware, but of all events shaping me sexually, this had the most impact. Sex was, therefore, a selfish individual act of self-gratification; relationships were fleeting; and there was the tendency to reduce women to objects to be conquered and used. Only a few years ago did I read about this whole (primarily male) phenomena in Donald Joy's *Men Under Construction*.

Life's challenge is that the sum of all of our experiences to date is who we are today. This background is taken with us each day, even into a marriage. With this resultant baggage it is relatively easy to understand the challenges that can be experienced. Our book, *Longing to Be Loved,* is about those challenges and our struggle to make our relationship work.

Several years ago Jill and I were asked to write on sex for Marriage Encounter. The question to which I was to respond was "How do I feel when you say no?" For many years this had been a real problem in our marriage. It wasn't until other changes in our relationship had occurred, and we had seen significant transformation, that we believed we could now attempt to dialog on this question.

As I picked up my pen to write, my mind quickly went back to those hurtful years. I wrote:

Dearest Jill,

In general, as I look back and think of our sex life, I feel sad. Sad, as I realize what a waste all those years we were "at war" were. No, we didn't use knives or guns, but the weapons we used were every bit as effective in wounding and maiming the opposition. Although "sticks and stones may break my bones, but names can never hurt me" may be the way the saying goes, the truth is that the *word* NO can hurt more and have longer reaching effects than physical abuse.

During that period of our marriage how I felt when you said no was where I lived my life. It wasn't the exception; it was the rule! I remember thinking, *Just what would it take to move the answer to yes?* My reactions ranged from withdrawing into my shell and feeling unloved and unappreciated to feeling defiant and thinking, *Well, if that's the way you feel, my needs can be met somewhere else!*

The longer things went on this way, the more I found myself focusing on what I wanted and on my needs. Then, out of frustration, I became busier and busier as I looked for other things to meet my need for belonging, love, and self-worth. As I focused more on self, any needs you might have had became secondary, and I would think, *I'm not getting what I expected out of this relationship. Something is going to have to change.*

I'm aware that many times I came across as demanding my rights. I guess this is where I see we lived our marriage for the first

12 to 15 years. The real wonder is that we are still together!

Now for the question: How do I feel when you say no? With all that as vivid memory, I'm really thankful for the changes in our lives. The last time I remember you saying no was several years ago and, as I recall, I was tired too, and it was no big deal. Your response to the change in my focus—from myself to you—has been phenomenal. I never dreamed such a "little" change could make such a "big" difference.

I really am thankful for you and the way you meet my needs. I never realized that the excitement of loving you just the way you are and trying to meet your needs to the best of my ability would bring such returns. I wish I had made the change years ago.

Thanks for being the best wife anyone could have!

Allan

Fortunately, the years since this rebirth have included much study and growth and sharing with others. An interesting facet of sexuality that is seldom touted is that several studies, including the famous *Redbook* study on sexuality, have shown that married Christian couples enjoy the highest sexual satisfaction.

JILL: My initial reaction to sharing my feelings on sex was "No way!" (I'm surely glad we don't have to give any presentations about sex.) We've had our difficult times, and I don't care if the world knows.

I figured we had come a long way in that area; we had at least discussed it! There was a time when we never shared physically, emotionally, or much of anything related to sex. Many times I thought, *If I keep Allan happy with other things, then everything will be OK.* I avoided sharing any of my feelings or needs with him.

When I was a child, sex was represented to me as a no-no. I grew up seeing little affection between my parents, and I knew of an aunt who slept around. Sex was portrayed as "dirty," something nice people didn't talk about—certainly not in public.

I have subsequently learned that my feelings were neither good nor bad. They just expressed who I was at that moment. My confidence in God and in Allan had been growing so that when we were asked to write on sexuality during Marriage Encounter, I was reluctantly willing.

I began my letter with a prayer: "Dear Father, Thank You for Your love that I feel. You know how difficult it is for me to relate to this thing called sex. Help me to do Your will. I need Your Spirit to guide my thoughts."

To the question of "How do I feel when I say no?" I wrote:

Dear Allan,

When I say no to your invitation to love, I feel guilty and scared. I have flashbacks of years past when we entered marriage unaware of each other's needs, and when I was so ignorant of a male's sexual drives and desires. I am reminded of my hurt, resentment, of feeling used, and of not communicating how I felt. I know I let you down when you needed me. What I'd really like to say is "I don't mind filling your needs if only you care enough to ask what my needs are."

I know that I did not always say no verbally, but I would conveniently arrange to spend time away from you in order to cope. My body language said, "Touch me not!"

Allan, as I empathize with your wounded feelings, I am reminded how much it hurts when others criticize and gossip about me. Recently someone took me aside and with a wagging finger in my face thoroughly chastised me. There was no understanding or sympathy, just judgment and condemnation. I was crushed.

Allan, I don't want you to feel bruised, wounded, and hurt as I felt that day. Your needs are important to me.

I love you,
Jill

Through all those years I felt wounded. I remember evening after evening, sitting on the stairs writing and watching for the lights to come up the long drive to our home. The house would be quiet with our little son tucked in bed. I hurt and felt forgotten because I didn't understand why Allan didn't let me know where he was at times, or how long his meetings would last. His business seemed not to be mine. Sometimes his words and looks would pierce me until I gave up, injured and confused.

On those stairs watching for the car lights, I wept, I prayed—sometimes I even sang. The song I liked best was "Something beautiful, something good; all my confusion He understood—all I had to offer Him was brokenness and strife, but He made something beautiful of my life."

The thought that God was still in control sustained me through those painful times. Yes, I have felt wounded, but now that we have learned to relate, I have been healed.

ALLAN: Each time we share I feel a lump come up in my throat. I realize that both of us were crippled, and each of us had inflicted wounds on the other. Oh, how many times I have praised God that He has taught us how to love unselfishly through humble service rather than hurting each other. We have been richly blessed!

JILL: By loving, by sharing openly and honestly, by listening to each other with our hearts, *healing has taken place.* Our experiences have brought us far beyond physical unity—we have gained emotional and spiritual oneness as well.

◆ ◆ ◆

This chapter ought to bring encouragement to any couple struggling with sexual difficulties. Don't give up! You can turn a conflicted sexual relationship into a fantastic one. Others have done it—so can you. Here are a few pointers:

1. *Sexual fulfillment requires sensitive and open communication.* Talk about this with your mate in a nonblaming manner. Husbands and wives must be able to share their deepest feelings about what pleases and delights them, and also about what displeases and frustrates them. They must be able to listen with encouragement, understanding, and caring to the feelings of each other.

2. *Get a good book on sexuality from a Christian perspective and read it aloud to each other, discussing it as you go.* You might investigate works by Alberta Mazat, Clifford and Joyce Penner, Nancy Van Pelt, and Ed and Gayle Wheat.

3. *Sex is not something that a man does to a woman; it is a sharing experience.* The satisfaction of the needs of one partner at the expense of the needs of the other partner is selfishness and exploitation. Both husband and wife must find satisfaction and fulfillment in the experience.

4. *Often the sexual needs of each partner may be different.* One may pos-

sess more sexual energy and, therefore, a desire for greater frequency than the other. Each mate may respond differently to such elements as time of day or night, romantic setting, creation of a mood or climate, or fatigue. These differences provide opportunities to practice unselfishness, communication, and loving concern for the needs of the other party.

5. *You may wish to let the woman take the lead, as if the two were riding bicycles together.* She is slightly in front, and he is careful to turn where and when she turns.

6. *Sexuality in marriage should not be viewed as some sort of performance that must measure up to a supposed norm or standard set by someone else (movies, novels, friends).* The couple should be able to enjoy each other and their own unique experience of oneness without disparaging comparisons. Orgasm should not be the goal. The experience itself should be meaningful and satisfying. You have shared a precious, intimate moment and glued your marriage more tightly together.

7. *What about those occasions when, because of illness, fatigue, distractions, etc., it really is necessary to say, "Not tonight, dear"?* The Kennedys, out of their rich experience, give us some good advice.

"In a loving and patient way, share your feelings about why this may not be a good time. Reassure your mate of your love so your lover will not feel rejected because of something he/she did. And set up an alternate time that is suitable for both. Be as courteous with your mate as you are when a friend asks you to dinner and you cannot make it. Ask for a rain check."

8. *Finally, pray about it together.* The spiritual connection is at the very heart of human sexuality. Ask God to help you be unselfish and sensitive to the needs of your spouse. Ask Him to bind you closer together through this experience. You can count on Him to answer. God cares about your sexual sharing. He made you for happiness.

Chapter 16

WHERE, OH, WHERE
DID OUR MONEY GO?

Shelly and Wayne's Story

*M*any years ago, when we were young, Tennessee Ernie Ford made a top-of-the-charts record about a poor laboring man who had to load 16 tons of coal each day. In spite of all his arduous work, he only got deeper in debt every day. He told Saint Peter that he couldn't answer the call to leave and go to heaven because he owed his soul to the company store.

Now, many years later, numerous couples can still relate to what it feels like to be deeply in debt. In fact, the PBS television program *Affluenza* stated that money plays a major role in 90 percent of divorces in the United States. Debt is a major problem in our society. Government economists estimate consumer debt in the United States to be over a trillion dollars. To put it another way, debt now amounts to 21 percent of disposable income.

How does money affect marriages? It can be a real point of disagreement. Couples can be in conflict when one wants to buy and the other wants to save. Unpaid bills create stress, especially when one partner blames his/her mate for running the family account into the red. Financial hardships fray nerves. An old proverb states that "when poverty comes in the door, love flies out the window."

What warning signs should admonish us that we are in the process of owing our soul to the company store? Two or more of the following should give us reason to take a serious look at our pattern of spending:

♦ Dipping into savings, or taking out loans to pay off old debts.

♦ Credit card cash advances and checking overdraft loans are rising.

♦ When large loan balances are paid off, similar debts are again incurred.

♦ The payment of only minimum due on credit card accounts.

♦ Second notices received on a number of debts.

♦ The delay of payments for essentials, such as utilities and health care, in order to pay credit card debts.

♦ Cancellation of credit cards by credit holders because credit limits have been exceeded.

♦ Monthly total due on various types of debt exceeds 20 percent of take-home pay.

—Adapted from "When the Debts Pile Up," *Better Homes and Gardens*, October 1985, p. 92.

Shelly and Wayne Perry share their own experience of dealing with mounting debt. Shelly is the director of field work in the Social Work Department, and Wayne is the director of physical therapy, both at Andrews University. What is particularly helpful is that they share the process used and its success in such a way that others who may be struggling with the same issue can follow the recipe. Shelly tells the story.

♦   ♦   ♦

We got married when we were young (21 and 23 years old). I was in the middle of college, and Wayne was to start his degree when I finished. When I completed my master's degree, we decided it was in our best interest to purchase a house. My parents were willing to let us borrow the down payment, but this rapidly added to our school loans and "other" bills, so we found ourselves deep in debt.

I, by nature, tend to be an extrovert. I like being around people and having fun. The down side of my personality is that I have a hard time staying focused on a goal, such as paying off bills and loans, because I don't see anything happening, yet I never seem to have money to spend. Fortunately, opposites attracted, and I married a man who is more introverted and goal-oriented. He realized that for us both to be focused on the goal of getting out of debt he had to make it real for me.

One day Wayne was "in the back room" paying the bills when he called me. He proceeded to show me a chart he had made on a large poster board. (I prefer things that are visually stimulating and interactive. A piece of paper would not have worked as well.) He had listed the loans we owed across the top, and the months down the side. The amounts with the highest interest were listed first.

Every month thereafter, while he was paying bills, he would call and give me a big red marker to put an X in one of the spaces provided. When the first account was paid off, the money set aside for that debt went toward the next bill on the list (yes, this was already figured in when he created the chart) and on down the table. We also would have a special celebration when a bill was paid off.

Our final loan was to my parents for the down payment on our house. We ended up being able to pay them $1,000 per month until our $10,000 bill was paid—an accomplishment I would have never dreamed possible. It was only by not elevating our pattern of living (we continued to live like students, even though I had a professional job), and having the "bill" money accumulate, that we were able to do it.

This method really helped me. We could see the end in sight. We became a team as we focused on our end goal. We celebrated our successes. We could discuss what we wanted to do with our money after a specific date instead of saying "once our bills are paid." People often say "once our bills are paid off" in the same manner as "let's get together for lunch sometime," when they both know it will never happen. Last, I could *see* where my hard-earned money was going. It didn't just disappear with the explanation "I had to pay bills."

◆ ◆ ◆

Joe Engelkemier, in an article entitled "Don't Worry About Money" (*Adventist Review*, Sept. 19, 1991, p. 16), states the following guidelines:

◆ Set aside tithe and offerings first (see the McNitt story, chapter 3, page 25, "The Couple That Prays Together," and how they were blessed).

◆ Become increasingly efficient at work (use time wisely).

◆ Save regularly (even if it's only a small amount at first).

◆ Use good judgment in food purchases (good nutrition does not require highly processed food).

◆ Limit your nonfood wants. "My God will fully satisfy every need" (Philippians 4:19, NRSV). Distinguish needs from wants.

◆ Avoid charge account debt. Charge only what you can pay off each month.

◆ Never buy impulsively.

◆ Pray as you shop.

◆ Dismiss worry. Do everything you can to be a good steward and leave the rest with God.

Some couples break up over money. The Perrys learned how to solve the problem together. Of course it wasn't easy. Of course it took restraint and even sacrifice. But being willing to communicate about it and being willing to focus their joint efforts on it brought satisfying success.

Chapter 17

TRIBUTE TO A MODEL

Louise and Richard's Story

Awise man (maybe Albert Schweitzer) was once asked about the most important rule for rearing children. He replied, "There are three of them: example, example, example!" His overemphasis makes a valid point. Often we need to see a good model before we know how to live a satisfying life.

Some years ago Roger was called to the faculty of a boarding academy. To get oriented, we arrived a little before school was to begin. We knew none of the students, although some community young people were around. On Sabbath we attended the academy church for the first time for worship. At the close of the service we walked out of the building, hand in hand. This was our usual practice, and we didn't think anything of it.

As we went through the door, we passed two young women. We

couldn't help overhearing one say to the other, "Look at that! I hope that happens to me someday." We've never forgotten that brief conversation, because it so indelibly implanted the value of modeling.

We've had many opportunities since then to see that demonstrated. People often grow up in homes where they have not witnessed the type of relationships that make good marriages. We have heard young people say, "I don't know anyone who is happily married." Making a good marriage does not come naturally. Couples need to see it demonstrated. How can one do something right if he or she has never seen it done?

The story in this chapter is not about seeing a happy couple model good marital behavior. It does deal with learning traits from a model and mentor that changed a rocky relationship into a great marriage. Louise and Richard Choi have opened their lives for the benefit of our readers. Richard serves on the New Testament faculty of the Seventh-day Adventist Theological Seminary at Andrews University. Louise is a surgical nurse at Lakeland Hospital in St. Joseph, Michigan. We find this story to be deeply moving. It has a sacredness about it. The Chois have displayed much courage in sharing these private memories. We can all benefit. Richard tells the story.

MEETING MY WIFE AGAIN FOR THE FIRST TIME

My wife and I have opposite personalities. In school I did well in literature and language; Louise did well in science and math. I am a hopeless romantic; Louise is a realist who lives with both her eyes open all the time. I enjoy spontaneity and a degree of chaos; Louise likes predictability and planning. I often lapse into daydreaming and sometimes even forget what time of the day it is; Louise is very focused. I like talking; Louise likes being at quiet with herself. We enjoy many of the same things in life, such as music, traveling, and religion, but the way we go about enjoying them could not be more different.

People say that opposites attract, and that seems to be what happened in our marriage. The irony is that when we first met in the summer of 1980, we were both convinced that we were the two most identical persons on earth. We thought that after getting married we were going to live the rest of our lives together, enjoying many of the same things the same way. Moreover, marrying a person of similar personality and background was extremely important for me, because I had read somewhere that marriage partners who were similar to each other tended to live happier and stay together longer. When I began dating Louise, I became convinced that I had at last found in her just such a person. Both of us were Korean-Americans who had come to America as teenagers. We were both third-generation Adventists who had grown up in supportive homes. We enjoyed many of the same things in life.

After we got married, however, it became evident that in our personalities there were sharp and seemingly irreconcilable differences. My cherished notion that I had to marry someone who was like me in order to succeed in marriage made this dawning realization especially painful. At first we went though a period of denial, but when our son was born just a year and a half into the marriage, we were no longer able to ignore the pronounced differences that existed between us. Between our jobs and the new baby, tension mounted; we often clashed over these differences.

Then help came from an unexpected source. About six months before we were scheduled to move back to Michigan to work on my Master of Divinity degree at the Adventist Theological Seminary, the lease ran out on the house we were renting in Burbank, California, and we were unable to renew it for the remaining time. This landed us in a terrible quandary. So we were very relieved and grateful when Louise's parents suggested that we live with them during this short interim—with all our belongings!

Inwardly, though, I was a little apprehensive about this new arrangement, because I thought that living with my in-laws might cause us to drift farther apart. Of particular concern was that both my wife's maternal and paternal grandmothers were living there also. Her maternal grandmother was about 86 years old, and her paternal grandmother was about 77 years old.

To my complete surprise, living with my wife's extended family for those six months turned out to be a real blessing. If it were not for that experience, we would not be enjoying the happy marriage we have today. Her parents lived in a four-bedroom house. They were kind enough to give us the largest room in the house. The room had been converted from a garage and had a separate door that led directly to the outside. What was especially nice about this room was that it had a separate bathroom. Living out of this room for the next six months and eating the food my wife had grown up eating, I was able to observe and experience the lifestyle and values that had shaped her. The whole experience was an eye-opener.

The most remarkable thing about her home was that it was a very quiet place. People spoke quietly and infrequently. Even with seven of us living there, hardly a sound was made throughout the day, other than the intermittent cries of our baby son. My home, where my mother had raised five of us unruly boys, was a place of loud talking and laughing, spontaneity and excitement, and often complete chaos. It resembled a gym more than a home. I must admit that I appreciated the quietness with which my in-laws went about their lives.

The person who had the deepest impact on me during this period was Louise's paternal grandmother. Her name was Bok Soon. I began noticing that my wife's values were in many ways those of her paternal grandmother, which in turn were the values of the Korean farming families. Even though her grandmother was diffident, like my wife, she shared with me many interesting and enlightening stories from her youth in Choon-Chun, South Korea. Particularly touching was the story of the day she gave birth to her first son, Louise's father.

It was early in the morning, and she was preparing breakfast for the whole extended family with her other sisters-in-law. In the old Korean culture, breakfast used to be the biggest meal of the day. She was feeling the contractions and knew that the baby was on its way. But she wanted to help make breakfast for the family and clean up before going away some place to have the baby. One of her sisters-in-law noticed that she was trembling and rushed her to a room where she gave birth to her first baby. It was not necessary for her to be in the kitchen that morning, but she had done it because she did not to want to cause any commotion before breakfast and bring inconvenience on the people of the house. If the ability to defer meeting one's own needs for the needs of others is a sign of maturity, then this was a remarkable show of maturity and a self-giving spirit from a girl who was then only 19 years old.

The more I listened to the grandmother's fascinating stories and observed her ways, the more I was impressed with the maturity of her character. During my entire stay I never once heard her complain or raise her voice at anyone or anything. There was never a trace of bitterness in her. This woman was remarkable in other ways, too. Raised on a farm, she was extremely handy and frugal. She even made her own soy sauce and brooms. Admiration led to emulation. I decided that these values were exactly what I needed in my life. In learning to admire this gentle older woman's agrarian virtues, I was falling in love with my wife's values.

One lazy afternoon in southern California, I was sitting at my desk, working on a presentation I was to give in a couple days. A rhythmic staccato of sweeping sounds came from the backyard. At first I didn't pay much attention to it, but as the sound continued, I looked outside. There was the grandmother, bent over, sweeping the old concrete slab just outside the glass doors of the living room. She was sweeping the porch with a broom she had made herself, held firmly in her gnarled brown hands. As far as I could see, there was really no need to sweep that porch. It was clean enough. But I knew that she had looked for and found a useful activity to fill a lull in her day.

This brief moment seems to have been etched in my memory forever. It somehow swept up into itself every value my wife stood and lived for—frugality, predictability, quietness, and hard work—and planted them in my heart.

❖ ❖ ❖

Let's face it: some couples are stuck in detrimental ways of relating. In spite of their desire for something better, they can't seem to break out of a pattern of relationships that may destroy their marriage. They need outside help.

This help may come from a Christian counselor, another couple who have discovered the prescription for a fulfilling marriage, or a trusted friend who will listen without judgment. The couple may be so emotionally close to the problem that they cannot think objectively. A neutral third party may be able to see destructive patterns that the partners cannot recognize. This intervener must not be someone who will take sides, tell the couple what to do, or gossip to others. What is needed is someone who loves both of them, who will gently lead them to find their own solutions, and who, most of all, will model how to live an effective Christian life.

The most reliable outside source, though, is God. He can melt hearts and give wisdom. However, He often ministers through other humans, as He did through Bok Soon. How wonderful to have a model and a mentor to whom we can turn in times of distress.

Chapter 18

THE UNEXPECTED ALMOST TRIPLETS

Audrey and Jim's Story

Children are a blessing from the Lord, yes, but . . . Let's admit it from the start. Children can be a major cause of conflict between couples in a marriage. This may begin with arguments over whether to have children at all, how many to have, and when to have them. One of the most prominent causes of disagreement in a marriage is over the discipline of the children. One parent may be lax, the other strict. Then there is the economic question. Children are very expensive. Government estimates on the cost of raising a child to the age of 18 run more than $225,000. Making ends meet can put a lot of pressure on a marriage. Then too, teenagers often break their parents' hearts by rejecting their values. Yes, children can fracture a marriage.

On the other hand, children can be the tie that holds a marriage together. They can provide a common cause around which parents can unite. They can bring responsibility to a home. They may call out the love, tenderness, and joy in the parents' lives that will overflow into the relationship between the spouses.

What makes the difference? A difficult question without a perfect answer. However, for starters both parents must truly love and desire children. They must be committed to the idea that children will enrich the marriage and the home. They must be flexible enough to roll with the punches and patient enough to keep steady in the inevitable hard times. They must be willing to sacrifice personal whims for the larger good of their offspring.

Audrey and Jim North epitomize this ardor. As they tell their story, one can feel the passion they have for their young ones. Through thick and thin this shining goal brought stability to their marriage. They will introduce themselves in the following story.

During our engagement and early marriage we spoke of having four children. After we were married on August 12, 1962, we moved into an apartment at Hinsdale Sanitarium while Audrey finished nursing school, and then into Garland A-15 at the seminary for the last year of Jim's Bachelor of Divinity program (now Master of Divinity). Since Audrey was working full-time, and Jim was studying full-time, having children had to take a backseat. Besides, the two of us were having a great first year of marriage. The pill did its job well.

But once we moved to Portland, Oregon, in July 1963, and our new married friends were having children, the satisfactions of having each other gave way to increasing longings to join the ranks of new parents. For some time we tried the natural method without success. We counted days. We were getting the days right. We took Audrey's temperature. Our timing was on target. But still the menstrual periods came. Sometimes our hopes rose during a few days delay, only to be dashed. Our anxiety began to mount.

So we went to a gynecologist who added fertility medication to supplement the natural method. All the while, we prayed for pregnancy. It seemed as though we were to be another Sarah and Abraham. Two years of trying seemed like an eternity to us. Prayer, nature, and medication all seemed fruitless. Jim was checked for sperm count. It was on the low side, but within a normal range. Nothing but a child would satisfy us, and nothing worked.

Sometime during our third year of marriage, the baby urges became so intense that we began to think about getting a baby through adoption. It seemed like every couple in our parish had children, or had a baby on the way. We just wanted a baby—by any appropriate means. We weren't quite as desperate as Abraham and Sarah. Besides, we weren't rich and had no maids. Actually, Abraham and Sarah's method of helping God never crossed our minds. If God was willing, we would adopt a child. Now that could work. Adoption satisfied all the criteria, except the child would not be born to us. But so what? We could help God without guilt.

The decision to adopt was not hard. As a matter of fact, neither of us had any reluctance about adoption. Jim had an adopted sister, who as a 3-month-old infant joined his family when Jim was 16 years of age. He also had a cousin who was adopted. When Jim's mother told him this early in his teen years, to his mind nothing about his cousin or his family changed. He was still Jim's cousin, any way he looked at it. Benjamin and Joy, his younger sister by birth, and Jim had enjoyed many great times together.

On January 31, 1965, one of Audrey's nursing coworkers told her about a Waverly Baby Home in Portland. We were there in a few days, making application for a baby—boy or girl, it mattered not a whit—when and if they acquired a baby. Did we care what its race was? No. We just wanted a baby. After making application, we returned home to continue child-trying—counting days and taking temps. But hope was remote; the prospects seemed distant so there were no preparations—no purchases of baby items, even gender neutral ones such as a bassinet and diapers.

In December Jim received a phone call from the National Service Organization at the General Conference. Clark Smith, the director, extended a call to Jim to fill a position as an Air Force chaplain. There was an urgency to the call. The General Conference had already lost one Air Force position because they couldn't find a pastor with all four qualifications—under 33 years of age at time of entry, two years full-time ministry experience, a B.D. degree, and ordained to the gospel ministry. Jim's was the only name they had for the remaining chaplain position. He met all qualifications except for ordination. They had two weeks to supply a candidate.

After praying and consulting with the senior pastor and conference president, we accepted the call. It meant that Jim would be ordained a year early. After about six months of processing he would enter the Air Force, go to chaplain school, and be assigned to some Air Force base. Initially it would be a three-year commitment with no strings attached. But what would be the response of the Waverly Baby Home director? With this kind of major change in location and vocation, would they still consider us appropriate parents for an orphan who needed a stable family? Of course we had to tell them. More prayer.

Surprise! On February 5, 1966, Waverly phoned with the news that they had a baby girl for us and that we could start the administrative process for adopting her. She had been born to teenage parents on December 20, 1965, and her name was Dawn. Did we still wish to adopt? The "yes" was out almost before the question was finished. A worker would visit us in the near future to assess our family situation and home. We needed to get a lawyer to assist in the adoption process. The cost would be the hospital bill for the birth, whatever legal costs we incurred, and a minimum $25 donation. We about went into orbit. Delight of delights! Hope sprang anew. We were ecstatic!

Later that month Audrey seemed to have come down with flulike symptoms—fever, a cold, and vomiting that she couldn't seem to shake. Six weeks later she went to the doctor. After a thorough checkup, we received another surprise—Audrey was pregnant and due in October. Should we still adopt? That was a dumb question! The two tots would be good company for each other. By God's grace we could handle it. We were young and afraid of nothing. Had we not accepted our first call to a ministry location 3,000 miles from our homes? (Audrey was from Brockton, Massachusetts, and Jim was from New York City.)

February was full of good news. Jim's ordination would be held on February 20 in the Sharon church, where he had been associate pastor for three and a half years. Both our parents came for that exciting and momentous event. We also had just arranged to purchase a new car. The windows of heaven had opened. A new and challenging ministry, ordination, two babies, a new car—what other good things could there be? Little did we know!

The social worker came to visit us and was very pleased with our home situation. The fact that we were entering the military was considered to be in our favor. The baby home had no reservations about the change in job or the change in location. They would help by speeding up the adoption! We checked with the conference. The treasurer would pay the hospital costs just as if the baby had been born to us! He would also pay the legal fees for the conference lawyer. The wheels began to turn.

Everything proceeded like clockwork. The ordination was a moving service. A General Conference representative, W. Eva Duncan, presided, assisted by the Oregon Conference president, H. L. Rudy. The conference secretary, Richard Schwartz; the pastor, A. Wellington Clarke; and Jim's father, James North, Sr., also took part. Jim's father had baptized him and performed Audrey and Jim's wedding. Now he was a part of Jim's ordination. The presence of Jim's mother and sister and both of Audrey's parents brought God, the church, and family together in a most significant way.

In May the baby home phoned one day with the news that we could come and see little Dawn. We went to see her the next day. She was so precious, with the cutest dimples and a heart-grabbing smile. The director asked us if we wanted her. It was love at first sight. Again, the "yes" almost beat the question. But what she said next caused our jaws to drop. We could take her home right then!

All we had was the blanket and the clothes she was wearing. So off we went with one in arms and one in the womb. On the way home we stopped at a supermarket and became the immediate laughingstock of the clerk and customers in the purchase line. We had a cart *full* of baby food, and only one tiny infant. But one look into her bright, smiling face won them all. In one moment we had gone from a couple to an adoptive family—with a lot of growing to do.

Jim was endorsed by the General Conference so that his military processing could begin. The exchange of paperwork, the security investigation, and the physical exam all proceeded with very minor delays. On June 6, 1966, Jim was sworn into the Air Force Reserve as a first lieutenant. Orders soon followed that he should report to the Air Force Chaplain School at Maxwell Air Force Base, Montgomery, Alabama, on Sunday, September 6. He would actually be considered active duty as of August 29.

In July we attended our first Seventh-day Adventist military chaplains conference in Wawona, Yosemite. Audrey was heavy with child. There were numerous comments about how big she was, and perhaps someone hinted at twins. But we paid no attention. We had renamed our daughter Stacey Marie, and all the chaplains and the wives who were there wanted to hold and carry her. She had a big, spontaneous, dimpled smile for everyone. She was the darling of the camp.

On August 29, after the government had packed and taken our household goods, we loaded our car and left Portland. Audrey's doctor had advised that we stop in places where there was a hospital. We were surprised at that advice. Audrey had noted that during her exams the doctor had listened in two places, but she paid no serious attention at the time.

With hardly a gasp, Audrey and Stacey boarded a plane for Boston. She was going to spend six weeks with her parents in Brockton while Jim was in chaplain school. When she got off the plane, her mother took one look and said, "Audrey, you are going to have twins." But Audrey paid no attention.

That was a Sunday. The following Friday night Audrey was plagued by "gas" pains while they attended an evangelistic meeting in Boston. She still had a month before delivery, but her wise mother persuaded her to go to the doctor. He was not available, but the hospital admitted her until he could see her in the morning. She had no clothes or anything with her, and the UNEXPECTED was about to happen. Sabbath morning the doctor took X-rays and came back with the news that there were *two* fetuses. A half hour later the delivery proved him correct!

Audrey's father phoned Jim with the news that afternoon, but since there was no emergency, he couldn't get away to see them until the following weekend. There they were in incubators, twin girls, a month premature—Amanda Ruth, three pounds eleven ounces, and Alicia Carrie, four pounds seven ounces. The windows of heaven had opened wide, and there was hardly room to receive all these blessings.

Jim graduated from chaplain school in mid-October and spent a few days in Brockton with his suddenly enlarged family. We had planned on two babies, then had three without warning within the space of eight months. Jim's assignment was to Amarillo, Texas, Air Force Base, so off he went to his new job. He couldn't take the family because of the segregated housing in Amarillo.

It took a month and many disappointing experiences to find a White owner who was willing to rent to a Black family. Again it seemed that getting prayer answered was a very daunting project, in spite of all the biblical promises. As usual, Jim spoke with the owner on the phone, mentioning nothing about racial origin. This woman showed the house cordially, as did all the others. But when faced with the question "May we rent this house?" she took a deep breath and said, "Well, we have never rented to Black people before, but I guess we will be willing to try." It was a beautiful three-bedroom house with a large fenced backyard in an all-White neighborhood. We are sure that this woman took a great risk.

On the way back to Brockton to pick up his family, Jim had to drive through a November snowstorm that closed the interstate for many miles. He stopped and slept in the car at a gas station just off the bypass in Indianapolis during the night. Fortunately, he had a duck down-filled sleeping bag that he had purchased for junior camp in Oregon. So in spite of below-freezing temperatures, the sleeping bag was sufficient. On the return trip the twins slept in the back seat, one in a bassinet and the other in a laundry basket, and Stacey sat in the lap of whoever was not driving. Clothes and belongings occupied every space, plus a full car-top carrier.

We stopped at our friend's home in Chicago. He lived near the University of Chicago, where persons watched for cars with out-of-state plates. While we ate dinner, someone broke into the car and stole quite a few clothes, including Jim's two new Air Force uniforms. We should have unloaded the car first. After that we stopped overnight at Air Force bases and spent hours washing and drying diapers.

After the family arrived in Amarillo, we never had a problem in our neighborhood, other than the fact that no one would speak to us except for the man who lived on one side of us, and the mail carrier. The neighbor offered to lend Jim his lawn mower, which Jim gratefully accepted. He would frequently converse over the fence. And the mail carrier rang the bell and spoke with Audrey every day.

We lived in that house for a year before base housing opened up, and we were blessed with four-bedroom quarters normally reserved for full colonels. The base was scheduled for closing in two years, and since people were leaving and not being replaced, this house came open, and there were no colonels, no lieutenant colonels, or no majors on the housing list.

God blessed this lowly young captain, his wife, and his almost triplets with it. The dining room was furnished with a large table and chairs that had beautiful white upholstery. There was also an expensive China hutch.

The 19 chaplains at Amarillo and their families, which included a Mormon and a Christian Scientist, were the finest of Christians. The other chaplains included Baptists, Methodists, Lutherans, a Disciples of Christ, a Presbyterian, and several Catholic priests, all Caucasian, but race was never an issue. When Jim first arrived, one of the Lutheran chaplains was assigned as his sponsor. He helped Jim with house hunting, and he became Jim's mentor and closest friend. His wife was very warm with Audrey. In 1971 we were again stationed together. The relationship grew. His wife and older children baby-sat our tiny ones.

Our greatest fun during those two years at Amarillo was meeting persons who always admired our "threesome." They would always ask, "How old are the girls?" For three months of the year they are the same age. At these times we would answer, "Two," or "Three." "Oh, they are triplets!" Our answer was, of course, no. It was most humorous to see the puzzled expression. Then we would end their suspense by telling our story of adoption and the birth of twins. God also blessed us with a handsome, energetic, and bright son in 1974.

As Paul wrote: "What shall we say then?" Our family has been through many trials, especially during the children's teen years and early 20s. But the "triplets" and our son have all become successes. Our oldest is a lawyer for the Department of Veterans Affairs. She is married and has three children. One twin is a staff accountant for a research firm. The other is the payroll manager for a large hotel. Our son is a physical education teacher for the male students of grades 1-12 at Bermuda Institute. Jim retired in 1986 after 20 years in the Air Force, finished his Doctor of Ministry at Andrews University, and was hired as a seminary professor at Andrews in 1988. Audrey is a nurse supervisor for the Area Agency on Aging in St. Joseph, Michigan.

Always, the grace of God is sufficient for all challenges. "Ask, and it shall be given you," "Good measure, pressed down, and shaken together, and running over" (Matthew 7:7; Luke 6:38).

Chapter 19

FIFTY YEARS OF LOVE AND LIFE TOGETHER

Elsie and Edwin's Story

*T*his story was written by Elsie Buck about a very trying and stressful experience that she and her husband lived through in the mission field. They have both devoted themselves in demonstrating God's love to all who touch their lives. Both are educators. Edwin is professor emeritus of Purdue University, where he taught for 24 years, and Elsie taught music in the St. Joseph Public Schools. In addition, she has given a lifetime to piano teaching, and continues to adjudicate for the National Guild of Piano Teachers.

❖　❖　❖

We were in college. It was wartime, and all around us the presence of conflict in the world touched our lives. Edwin had come from Detroit to prepare for the ministry, and I, coming from a junior college in the South, was majoring in music and now finishing my senior year on June 6, 1943. We were young. I was 20, Edwin 22. We had been going together for a year and a half before our wedding day and had the joy of youth and love in our hearts.

We were married the same day on which I received my Bachelor of Arts degree, and after Edwin's graduation we were asked to join the Michigan Conference of Seventh-day Adventists in pastoral work. We spent several months working with M. L. Venden, a major evangelist of that era. Then we worked with several small churches that needed a young pastor, and spent a special year teaching at Cedar Lake Academy before being appointed to the Mount Pleasant district in the center of the state.

In Mount Pleasant we had to build a new home, inasmuch as there was no other available housing for a family of five so soon after the close of World War II. Our three small children needed space for themselves and a yard for play. A new home would give them all they needed in those tender years of life and would allow us an environment from which to serve the new church appointment and the community in this university town.

And yet, it was not to be.

A call came from the General Conference of Seventh-day Adventists one fall day that asked us to go to India to Vincent Hill School and College, in Mussoorie, to become the pastor and to teach classes in religion for those focusing on service for the English community in India. Partition, as it was called—the separation of India from English rule—had occurred in 1947, and the English-speaking presence of many in the country demanded schools and colleges where the English language continued to be used. Vincent Hill School and College was thus an integral part of the educational system for the church and a service for the missionaries who sent their children, even for the elementary grades, to Mussoorie for their education under the tutelage of dedicated teachers.

After two months on the high seas in a freighter, the M.S. *Borneo,* we arrived in Bombay. Then by train and bus, we traveled to Mussoorie, our destination high in the foothills of the Himalayan Mountains. Riding in a rickshaw, we continued onto the mountainside campus of Vincent Hill, where we were to be for the next six years.

Those six years in India were to open windows of life that we had no idea we would experience. We were to be touched by many joys and many heartaches as well. And how does one survive when told that one's husband will not live through a dreadful case of infectious jaundice? How will one manage alone, with three children, in a foreign country without the presence of a husband and a father? Let me share with you how God provided for us in this medical emergency.

In addition to our teaching responsibilities at Vincent Hill, another phase of our experience in India was the invitation to be involved in evangelistic outreach during the winter vacation months of December, January, and February. This was always a time of discovery, of anticipation, of faith, and of appreciation for God's mercies and goodness.

It was 1953, and a new school year was about to start. We had spent several weeks in New Delhi in an evangelistic outreach for the people of the city. It was there that our family was exposed to infectious jaundice—a disease that attacked Edwin with a serious case of fever, loss of appetite, and a telling yellowing of the skin that revealed a severe case of hepatitis A. What does one do when life becomes fragile, and nothing seems to improve the declining strength and vitality of the one you love?

The situation was serious. Every effort was made to minimize exposure to others. The two older children were placed in respective dorms on campus, and visitors were not allowed to come to our home. During these weeks of illness Edwin was bedridden and unable to teach. There he was—quiet, thin, disconsolate, with no healing in sight. The days were long, very long, for him and for me. With a heavy heart I continued my teaching of music and piano in another building, and we had to plan for others to care for our little 5-year-old boy.

Week after week the disease progressed. What could we do? How would we save Edwin's life—the life that was so precious to me and to the children? I asked myself that question again and again, pleading with the great Healer of all time—our Lord—for help, for direction, for a miracle. We had always been a praying family. Service in God's vineyard was the focus of our lives. Was our service to be cut short by this illness? I continued to plead with God for Edwin's life, as did many, many others, friends far and near.

Then one day God brought an incident to my remembrance. A year or so before a missionary doctor had given us samples of a new medicine that was being used in the United States. As he shared it with us he said, "Just in case you need something new, of great power and help." Under the intensity of our situation, however, until that moment those pills (a new antibiotic) and their presence in our home had been forgotten.

But suddenly that morning God brought them to our attention. We asked the local doctor if we should use these pills. He wasn't sure they would help, but said, "Try them."

And we did. We earnestly prayed and anxiously waited. After a few days Edwin 's appetite returned. Slowly at first, then day by day, Edwin's health began to improve. With his appetite returning he began to gain weight. He could now drink water and retain it, and little by little he was able to retain food, all of which for months past he could barely absorb. He had lost 80 pounds during these months and now was in desperate need of the vital nutrients that his body had lost. The normal color of his skin tissue began to return—the yellow faded daily. We knew that a miracle was taking place, changes unheard of during the preceding weeks were now happening. This was a time of healing that led to a total restoration of health and strength.

Yes, a miracle had taken place.

In all the years since that time of intense trauma and suffering, Edwin has not experienced any damage to the liver nor to any other part of his body. Healing was complete—all in answer to prayer and God's immense power to heal and to restore life to one who had suffered so much. We look back on that time of great distress for our family and raise our voices in praise to the One who heard our prayers and who led in the healing process of one so close to death.

The partnership of marriage relies on love, on commitment, on dedication in times of joy and in times of perplexity. During this difficult time it took all three—love, commitment, and dedication. We realized ever so more deeply how precious we were to one another after coming so very close to losing each other. I can never forget how much I cherished Edwin's life—a life that God snatched back from the brink of death.

Even above all these there is one aspect of marriage that superseded all others—the time of prayer a couple spends together, a time of sharing God's grace in their lives and His power to lead, to heal, and to restore. As a result of this experience we were impressed with two great truths—

God's love for us, and our love for each other.

Prayer is the key in the hand of faith that helps make a marriage last.

◆　◆　◆

Elsie has so poignantly written their love story, which began with the romantic-idealistic DREAM stage. As all committed married couples do, she and Edwin must have worked through the next two stages: DISILLU-SIONMENT (when the faults of each other become a challenge to live with), and then on through DISCOVERY (when the strengths instead of the faults) come into focus, to the reward for persevering, which becomes DEPTH, the stage of mature love. This fourth stage of love is far more en-during, meaningful, and fulfilling than the DREAM stage of untried love.

When two young starry-eyed people say their marriage vows and promise to stay by through sickness and health, they usually have no con-ception of what illness could mean in their relationship or that it could ever happen to them. A long, serious illness can place a very challenging strain on any relationship. The person who is ill can become depressed, critical, irritable, and no longer able to relate. The caretaker may become so overwhelmed with taking care of the ill spouse, plus carrying the duties of both persons, that he/she decides to leave the marriage.

On the other hand, as in the case of Edwin and Elsie, the crisis can pull them closer together. In the words of Patrick Morley, they adapted in this manner: "When the body of the wife is sick, so is the body of the hus-band. They are one flesh. When the body of the husband takes ill, so does the body of the wife. They are one flesh. We belong to each other, as we belong to the Lord. How important it is for your mate to have an assur-ance that you will be there in the dark hour of illness" (*Two Part Harmony* [Nashville: Thomas Nelson, 1998], p. 17).

Edwin recently had his turn at being the caretaker when Elsie needed major surgery for a hip replacement. As in the previous illness, the same coping skills prevailed, that of lots of love and patience, dedication, and much prayer for divine guidance. Difficult times will come and go in any relationship. They can make or break the couple. The grace of God will make it a positive, growth-inducing experience.

Chapter 20

OUT OF THE SHADOWS

Anonymous

*I*f a marriage is to survive and flourish, it must be based on openness. Scripture reports of that first happy couple in Eden that they were "naked . . . and were not ashamed" (Genesis 2:25). To the extent that husband or wife withdraws, the marriage is in jeopardy. Secrets from life before marriage, kept hidden deep within, may well prove a barrier to the open communication that is desired in a fulfilling marriage. One of the characteristics of a lasting marriage is that the couples trust each other with everything.

The story that illustrates this truth was shared with us by a young woman who came for counseling sessions to the Andrews University Counseling Center. She also attended a group conducted at the center by the same counselor, Peggy. After experiencing the healing touch of Jesus, she feels called to minister and encourage other persons who have been through a similar experience. She will remain anonymous to our readers in order to protect the privacy of her family. Her story is presented in her own words.

❖ ❖ ❖

BREAKING THE SILENCE

Marriages are breaking up, and many times people don't really understand the reason why. Sometimes traumatic experiences have happened to people, and if they don't get the right help to process and work through them, their marriage relationship may be doomed.

I have been married for three wonderful years to a wonderful man. To me he is a gift from God, because he is so loving, affirming, and supportive. With all these qualities that many a woman would want in her life, I felt unhappy, void, disgusted with myself in the sexual area, and immensely guilty.

For 20 years I was a good actor, playacting multiple roles. I could be the friendliest individual, the life of the party, and still feel a void. I would wake up after sleeping 10 hours and couldn't understand why I felt so exhausted. My husband would comment that I appeared to be sleeping soundly, in fact snoring, but my mind was constantly racing while I was asleep.

Prior to this period of my life, sleep had been an escape for me, because no one knew what I was thinking and feeling. But all this changed when I began having flashbacks from a childhood experience during which I witnessed my sister being raped by my father. (My father thought I was asleep.) I had repressed this memory for 20 years and had never told a soul.

In order to hide my true feelings, I outwardly acted happy and carefree. I felt guilty because I was hiding this dark experience from my husband. I knew that I was not open and honest with him, while he was open and honest with me. My husband knew something was bothering me and would ask me about it. I would skillfully change the subject so he wouldn't know that I was hiding something from him.

Emotionally, I began to withdraw from him, and from men in general. I felt I was being deceptive, yet I felt betrayed by my father who was regarded as a good man in the church. I wondered if all men were capable of this sort of behavior. The more my husband tried to understand me, the more I worked at not being understood, saying that my hormones were at fault and that I was missing home and my family. I was afraid that if he should find out what was really bothering me, his feelings toward me would change.

A metaphor that would describe what I was feeling goes like this: My problem started out as a small sore that developed into an abscess. Left untended, it became gangrenous and, eventually, cancerous. It was a disorder that worked itself from the inside out and was destroying me in the process. I could no longer control the sleepless nights, the uncontrollable crying, the guilt feelings, the terrible shame, because I had done nothing to help my sister. I had remained silent throughout my childhood, pretending that I didn't know about the incident.

My husband recognized my need for psychological help when I told him that something had happened in my family that I just couldn't talk about but that was bothering me greatly. Eventually he persuaded me to seek the help of a Christian counselor. Going to the counselor's office was my longest journey. I wondered, *What will my counselor think of me? She might recognize my family, and the secret would be out. I could be wasting her time by making a big deal of something that happened 20 years ago.*

Saying that counseling changed my life sounds like a cliché, but it isn't. *It is absolutely true!* I felt as if I had walked out of a dust bowl into purified air. It was like leaving a hot stuffy room and walking out into a beautiful spring day and breathing in the crisp, clean air and feeling invigorated. This is the change that counseling with the Lord's healing produced in me.

Looking back, I feel pain for the 20 years I suffered. Why? Because I didn't tell a single soul about the pain. Not even my sister, who was the victim. It's like I became mute to that decade of my life. Being able to talk about the experience for the first time was more than a load off my back. Eventually I received the courage to tell my husband when my counselor assured me that my husband would understand and not blame me.

So I came home from a counseling session and said, "Honey, I have something I want to tell you." And I told him about this traumatic experience. To my surprise, he didn't seem surprised. He said, "I had an idea that it was something sexual, but I realized that by trying to find out, I was making you more distressed." He hugged me and held me, and then said, "I love you." That was the greatest affirmation!

Dealing with my true feelings was very difficult. The pain and the hatred I had been storing rose to the surface. At the same time I felt free to say no and not feel guilty. I could express my true feelings without being so concerned about pleasing others. This was so new to me because I had not expressed my true feelings for 20 years.

The rainbow didn't come immediately. Many prayers and tears, support from my spouse, counseling sessions, attending a recovery group, and the will to work on getting better helped me work through the anger, pain, guilt, and shame issues. The group experience took me back to my childhood when a group of us girls would go to a cozy place and play games. We were happy; we were together; we had a purpose. In the group I felt as if we could be ourselves with no need to hide. It was a relief!

THE PAIN OF PRETENDING

Before my recovery, when I felt angry about the traumatic experience, I took out my feelings on my husband simply because he was a man. I would blame him for anything, and this hurt him. He felt he was just not good enough because I was blaming him. The truth of the matter is that I felt *I* was not good enough. I didn't understand how discouraged my spouse had become because of my conflicted emotional state. He didn't know if he was loved or hated, and he needed to be told that he wasn't to blame. I felt I had to perform my marital duties, because that was what I was expected to do.

Since counseling I realize that I couldn't hide behind that experience. I had to face the truth. The truth was that I was hurting. Looking back at that point in my marriage, I realize that we argued frequently. Now I can talk honestly about how I feel. I no longer experience the shame and the guilt. I sleep soundly without the silent nightmares of before. I am being true to myself and to society. I have a closer relationship with the Lord. I'm a happier person and realize contentment. I have a fulfilling sexual relationship, with no strings attached. I have fun in my life! I can now talk freely about my journey. I can encourage others to seek help. Before, I was guarded and felt fear and shame if incest was mentioned. Before, I wanted to protect my family and the church by pretending it had never happened.

My journey continues. Going home and talking with my family was always a future plan, a daunting thought, but I knew I needed to do it so I could be completely free. A few weeks before I was leaving for vacation and home, my spouse and I sat down and discussed how I should approach the matter. Once again, getting started was the most difficult part of the journey. I worried about what they would think, because I'd always been a people pleaser. I wondered if they'd wonder why I needed to bring this up now when things had become so "stable." Nevertheless, I knew it had to be done.

Our vacation at my home was almost over. With my husband's encouragement I called my mother and sister to the room. I felt a surge of fear rise up in me, but I had come too far to turn back. I asked my husband to introduce why they had been called together. He stated that I had witnessed a traumatic event 20 years before that had severely impacted my life.

I continued the story. "Remember when— The reason I'm sharing this with you is because I've suffered feelings of guilt, blame, shame, and sadness for 20 years. I don't want to live my life like this anymore. I had the privilege of working with a counselor who has enabled me to come to this point." I began to cry and said, "It's tough, but I have to tell you how sorry I am."

My family surprised me. They said, "We don't blame you." My sister said, "I have put that behind me." I wondered how she, the victim, could put it behind her, while I had been carrying it for so long. They were so warm and understanding, and not at all as I expected. I know the Lord went before me. It dawned on me that they had moved on years ago, while I had stayed in the same place for 20 years. This experience freed me immeasurably. I felt more than elated when I saw how forgiving my family was and how happy they were.

I strongly advocate Christian counseling for persons who have suffered sexual abuse. I learned that with forgiveness comes healing. Before this experience I felt that I could never forgive. But I learned how to forgive and what forgiveness really meant—that I could move on with my life and be happy again. I know much healing has taken place, because now I am able to help other women who have been through this type of experience.

I can even say I'm thankful for this experience of so long ago, because it has taught me to rely solely on the Lord. Anything that has been fractured can be mended by His hand. I never thought I'd be able to say this, and I am amazed at God's healing power. This has given me a new purpose in life: to help others who have been through what I have experienced.

It is widely reported that one in five young women have experienced some type of sexual abuse by the time she reaches college. Many are fearful to let anyone know about the abuse because, unfortunately, they feel the shame the perpetrator should be feeling. This makes it difficult to seek counseling so they can work through the trauma. It also makes it difficult for them to relate sexually with their husbands. If you know someone who needs help moving from being the victim to being a survivor, God can use you as the bridge between the injured one and professional help. You may need to go with her to set up the first appointment with a Christian counselor.

An excellent resource for those who have suffered this trauma and for counselors is the Heitritter and Vought's book, *Helping Victims of Sexual Abuse: A Sensitive Guide for Counselors, Victims, and Families.* This is the book used with this young woman during her counseling sessions and that she and scores of others have found so helpful.

The Pacific Union Conference has published three excellent pamphlets on this topic: *Help for the Person Who Has Been Sexually Abused, My Child Has Been Sexually Abused,* and *Ministering to the Sexually Abused.* All this material is available from AdventSource, 1-800-328-0525.

Chapter 21

FOR BETTER OR WORSE . . .
TILL DEATH DO US PART

Stella and Berkeley's Story

Sometimes life simply caves in—everything seems to go wrong. And just as you come reeling back from one blow, something else hits you on the head. You go through the heartbreaking experience of being "dumped" by your mate and suffer the loss of self-esteem that event entails.

Then you find wonderful happiness in a new relationship.

But just as things seem to be looking up, a new and terrible crisis clobbers you. Can this marriage be saved? Will life ever seem normal again? Is there any hope in your future?

This is the story that Stella Freeman shares. Stella manages the bookstore at the Kettering College of Medical Arts near Dayton, Ohio. Berkeley is the southwest Ohio representative for Christian Record Services (a ministry to those who are blind). What they have been through would destroy

stroy many a marriage. But they, with the Lord's help, have learned to cope. Hopefully, their experience can encourage all of us "marrieds" to stick it out through trials and find the light at the end of the tunnel.

◆　◆　◆

"Till death do us part" were the words I said two days before my nineteenth birthday to the man with whom I was to spend the rest of my life.

But that life lasted only 10 years. After eight unsuccessful years of trying to start a family, a hysterectomy at the ripe old age of 28, and the murder/suicide of family members, my husband decided the grass had to be greener on the other side of the fence. He left with my best friend on Mother's Day, 1978.

Our divorce was final on what would have been our tenth anniversary. Over the next nine months I took him back on five different occasions. He seemed sincere and, after all, I did promise before God that "for better or worse, till death us do part." Each time we talked I would get my hopes up that our love would survive, and then he was gone again. After a three-month hiatus, I phoned and asked if he would meet me for lunch. We talked like old friends, but something was missing. I had forgiven him, and I still loved him, but I realized I wasn't in love with him. It was my thirtieth birthday. The healing had begun.

The church I grew up in was small, and there were no single men. I really wasn't interested in getting involved with someone who didn't belong to the same church I did, so I just accepted the fact that I might remain single. I prayed that if this was what the Lord wanted for me, then I would rejoice in my singleness.

Meanwhile, 50 miles away a good friend of my cousin had gone through a similar situation and also found himself single again. We had been casual church friends when we were both members of the Young Marrieds' Club several years earlier. After lots of coaxing from my cousin and several other friends, I phoned to invite him to Sabbath lunch. He politely refused my invitation, saying the singing group to which he belonged had a concert.

I didn't need a brick to fall on my head. "He's not interested," my low self-esteem told me. After all, I was now a divorced woman—damaged goods. I must have done something to cause my husband to turn to another woman.

What little self-esteem I had left took a nosedive.

Our church was holding evangelistic meetings, and I volunteered to help out. I had no family at home to take care of, so why not put my energy into helping with attendance records and other duties as needed? I didn't want to sit home and feel sorry for myself.

During one meeting we had a special treat. A gospel singing group was coming to put on a mini concert. I was especially excited since my cousin was a member of this group, as well as his now-divorced friend, Berkeley.

The group arrived in vans and planned to leave as soon as their part of the service was over. However, I volunteered to take anyone home who wanted to stay for the meeting. Imagine my surprise when Berkeley accepted my offer, and as soon as the meeting was over we began the 50-mile drive to his hometown. I think we learned more about each other during that short ride than many couples do in months. By the time we arrived, we both knew we wanted to pursue this friendship.

The next seven months were spent getting to know each other. We learned how much we had in common as we listened to each other. And when Berkeley proposed, my "yes" came without hesitation. I had been single for more than four years and felt ready to make that life-long commitment again. I found that his strength in people skills compensated for my shyness. Likewise, my strength in details compensated for his I-never-balance-my-checkbook laid-back style. We were married five months later.

The next two years were perfect. Our first argument didn't come until way past our anniversary. Even then we had determined not to "let the sun go down" until we had resolved our differences. Life on this earth just couldn't have been any better.

"For better; for worse!" I had experienced the *better* for more than three years, and then little things began to happen that sent me spiraling toward the *worse*.

My husband began to lose touch with reality. He would sometimes be so deep in his thoughts that he was nearly oblivious of what was going on around him. He became so disoriented that he had to take a medical leave of absence from his job. He spent three weeks in the psychiatric unit of a medical center, where he was diagnosed with obsessive-compulsive disorder (OCD) and clinical depression.

We went from the happiest days of our lives to a nightmarish existence. Every waking moment was spent dealing with his OCD. At home I answered hundreds of "what if?" questions, tried to quiet periodic crying spells, and kept the bills paid. At work, I worried that his mental state would cause him to put an end to his suffering with suicide.

I prayed continuously that the Lord would take this burden from us, or at least help us to cope. I knew He wouldn't allow more than we could bear, but that was little comfort at a time when my husband needed me for everything, and I was almost spent.

I began to wonder if love and commitment were enough. Then the words spoken at our wedding came through loud and clear: "For better or for worse; in sickness or in health." I'm not usually a quitter, so I took a long look at the past few years:

◆ The Lord brought us together.

◆ He provided a good job.

◆ He helped us meet our financial obligations during the 18-month disability.

◆ He never stopped loving us, even when we doubted Him.

How could I give up now? "Just a few more days, Lord. You've seen me through this far."

The changes began. They were slow but steady. The right combination of medications, therapy, patience, and prayer put us back on the road to the marriage we had envisioned and enjoyed.

I'm not going to say that life has been perfect. We still cope with the usual things married couples face—finances, differing opinions, etc., as well as an illness that is ever present in a lesser degree. Since his recovery 12 years ago, Berkeley has been working for one of our church ministries. He feels this is a small token for all that the Lord has done to sustain us through some very difficult times.

I think that if we had not made our vows before God I would not have felt the commitment to endure the hardships. It would have been so easy to walk away when times got tough. Then I think of all the good times I would have missed. Our love is stronger. We know we can depend on each other through trying times, and the Lord has blessed us more than we deserve.

For better or for worse; in sickness and in health; forsaking all others . . .
till death do us part.

◆ ◆ ◆

Wow! What a story! How did they do it? How did they survive—and even flourish—when everything was going wrong? How did they find their way back to peace and happiness? Notice again Stella's summary: "The right combination of medications, therapy, patience, and prayer put us back on the road to the marriage we had envisioned and enjoyed." Yes, patience and prayer! May the Lord grant it to each of us.

Did you catch this line from Stella: "I think that if we had not made our vows before God I would not have felt the commitment to endure the hardships."

Vows of commitment before God . . . They carried the Freemans through. They can do the same for each of us.

Chapter 22

WORK AT IT!

Carolynne and Bob's/Mary Sue and Francis's Story

*H*ere is a marriage myth that certainly needs to be debunked:

A couple falls in love. They are well suited to each other—common interests and all. Parents and friends approve. They marry in a joyous ceremony. They now have it made. A good marriage unfolds as naturally as a budding rose. They will automatically live happily forever after.

As our pastor, Dwight Nelson, would say, "Wrong! Wrong! Wrong!" While marrying the "right person" is a good start, connubial bliss is a daily work project. Like sanctification, it is the work of a lifetime.

There is the story of a woman who had been separated from her husband for six months and came to a counselor for help. "Tell me," she asked the counselor, "will I ever find anyone who will fit into my lifestyle so well that we won't have problems?"

When the counselor said no (the only honest answer), the woman mused, "Well, then I might as well start working on my present marriage. What must I do first?" Putting her shoulder to the wheel, she started in. The couple was reunited and patiently worked out a satisfying relationship.

The law of atrophy says that anything left to itself deteriorates. Gardens not tended are soon overrun with weeds. Muscles not used become flabby. A house not painted or otherwise preserved begins to peel and rot. So it is with marriage. Without constant daily attention and effort it will begin to go downhill. Couples begin to drift apart, and even if the pair stays together in the same house, all sense of intimacy may be lost.

Marriage contains the possibility of growth. It can get better every year with the deep passionate love and understanding of the golden years, far surpassing the romanticism of youth. How does this happen? You have to *work at it*. It will take intentional effort every day of the couple's common life. Frankly, it won't be easy, but the payoff will far exceed the effort.

One phase of this labor is what we call affirmation. This means expressing appreciation for one's spouse often—ideally, several times a day. Our human tendency is to criticize someone when he or she does something that we find annoying. Criticism always drives people on the defensive and damages the relationship. Affirmation, on the other hand, focuses on the positive traits and builds the sense of oneness.

Affirmation is especially effective when given in the presence of others. When we hold a marriage seminar we always end with a special celebration. First, we have a simple agape supper. Then we push back from the table and say, "Now is the opportunity to tell your mate what you appreciate about him or her." We offer to go first so that they can see how it is done. After we tell each other before these witnesses what we love and admire about each other, we sit down and say, "Now it's your turn."

One by one, people arise to declare their devotion for their partner. The room seems to glow. Tears flow freely. Hugs and kisses are given. The theme might well be "Can you feel the love tonight?"

We include two stories in this chapter. Neither case faced serious marital problems. They *prevented* them from occurring by working at their marriage, including the use of lots of affirmation. Notice that part of their secret of success is saying "I love you" several times daily.

◆ ◆ ◆

Bob and Carolynne Fetke share pastoral ministry in the Carolina Conference of Seventh-day Adventists. More importantly, they share a life together. Bob tells the story.

IN MINISTRY TOGETHER

On Mother's Day, May 13, 1973, Carolynne and I were married. It was an outdoor wedding on the campus of what was then called Southern Missionary College, or old SMC, to us alumni. We've enjoyed 27 years together and plan on continuing forever. What has been our marriage method of staying together? All along, we have been in the "Lord's work" together. We're still "in ministry" together. So working for the Lord, making His goals our goals, and serving His church has united us.

But we have learned! Yes, we've learned that being in the Lord's work together doesn't guarantee marital success. We've learned that when a good share of our dialogue and communication was about our work in the church that we'd better communicate about other things as well. We've learned that a good marriage, like anything else worth keeping, needs to have a lot of work. We've learned that we had to work on building up our marriage in all of its varied facets.

Therefore, in our married life we have enthusiastically attended programs such as Marriage Encounter, Intimate Life (based on Galatians 6:6), Romance at the Ranch at our summer camp, and any other special marriage enrichment weekends. Our priorities have been God first, our marriage second, our kids third, and our church fourth.

We've read good books together that seek to enrich marriage and have done the little exercises in those books. We've learned that our emotions are very important. We try to communicate and to understand one another's feelings and to tell each other everything. Even if others flirt with us, we divulge that to each other. My closest emotionally involved significant other is my spouse!

We try to keep our "childish" playing together fun and spontaneous. We've had our difficulties, but through honest exchange in love and prayer we somehow get through it. We say "I love you" often—first thing in the morning and last thing at night. We've been the couple who has everything but money, so we count our blessings.

We try to have a date night at least once a month. It may be as simple as eating out and going to Wal-Mart, or maybe driving to the big city mall near us. We use little sign languages of love, "our secret code," to each other. We believe that "absence makes the heart grow fonder," so if we're separated for several days, it is OK, because we have total confidence and trust in each other. We enjoy our phone calls and look forward to being together again.

Although we've both changed over the years, we appreciate more the good qualities of each other and what we both bring to our marriage. We've had wonderful role models, in that both sets of our parents have had lasting, committed marriages. Even if they hadn't, we know other people who have had wonderful unions, and we can model after them. We are thought of as a united couple—Bob and Carolynne go together like bookends. We aim to keep it that way and continue to be a blessing to all.

❖ ❖ ❖

Francis and Mary Sue Wernick have had a long and productive life together. Francis served as a pastor, and then moved into administrative work, including being president of the Lake Union Conference and a vice president of the General Conference. Mary Sue has been at his side all the way. Now retired, they still share in ministry together. Francis tells the story.

PARTNERS IN THE MINISTRY OF OUR LORD

It has been long recognized in Seventh-day Adventist ministry that two working together are more effective than one. Marriage is an important factor in successful ministry. When Mary Sue and I entered the gospel ministry in 1942, we were impressed that the call was for both of us. Our first place of work after leaving Union College was North Dakota. The years since have been adventuresome yet enriching.

The first place we called home was one room in the home of a lovely Lutheran family. With a salary of $22.50 per week (no rent subsidy), one room was all we could afford. After a few months we were able to rent two rooms, using one as a kitchen and the other as the bedroom. But we didn't mind such limited circumstances. After all, we were working for the Lord, and that was what counted most.

We went everywhere together. We gave Bible studies, held public meetings, and visited homes together. Years later we met a dear lady with whom we had studied the Bible during that first year and who had been baptized soon after by the conference president. What a reward for our work that year! There have been others, too, that we have met.

After 60 years of marriage, three children, and six grandchildren later, we both look back and marvel at the blessings of God and the privilege of working together. Of course, there have been times of stress. No marriage is totally free of stress and misunderstanding. However, because we both felt that we had been called to serve our Lord in His ministry wherever that might take us, the stresses became minor bumps in the road of life. They paled into insignificance in the light of the joys of ministry.

Our work has led us from pastoral ministry to administrative ministry and, finally, to retirement. Each step of the way it was important that we be together in the work we were doing. As the years went by the children came into our lives, and we couldn't go everywhere together as we had in the early years. But without the team, the ministry I was doing would have been much less effective. And when travel became part of the work I was called to do, the patient endurance of Mary Sue became as important as my work. Coming home to a place of refuge was terribly important to my peace of mind and effectiveness.

Finally, retirement became a reality. Knowing when to retire is important too. There are many ministries available to those in retirement. These would be missed if retirement comes when one is too ill to participate in them. We have found joy in the senior years.

And now, memories of past work bring joy to us. Not long ago we participated in the fiftieth anniversary of the opening of a church school. This took us back to a time when the church involved felt unable to begin a school. However, courage on the part of a few energized the rest of us, and the school was built and has been going ever since. We felt glad that we had been the pastoral couple when the school began in 1950. It was such a joy to see the enthusiasm for the school after 50 years.

Reflecting on the many years that have passed since the two of us began our ministry, we think the greatest lesson that we have learned is the importance of singleness of purpose on the part of both partners in marriage. The call to ministry is most effective when both feel God wants them to serve together, though how that is achieved may differ somewhat. We are grateful that God has permitted us to touch many lives for Him over the years, and some day we look forward to a reunion of many for whom we have labored.

◆ ◆ ◆

What can we learn from these two dedicated couples about making a good marriage into a fantastic one as the years go by?

We must work at it. Nothing worthwhile ever comes easy. People put tremendous effort into being successful at their jobs or professions. And next to our relationship with God, nothing in our lives is more important to health and happiness than the state of our marriages and the atmosphere in our families.

Constantly seek better ways to communicate. Learn how to be vulnerable and share our deepest feelings. Learn how to listen, not only to the words, but to the emotions behind those words.

Continually study how to be better partners. The Fetkes attended various seminars. They read books together. Working like this demonstrates that they mean business. They take marriage seriously.

Play together—do fun things together. A husband doesn't spend most of his recreational time out with the "boys." A wife doesn't spend hours socializing with other women. In satisfying marriages couples usually don't take separate vacations. They love to spend time together. They still date. They are each other's best friend.

These two couples found oneness in serving the Lord together. While not every couple can have joint occupations, each should do some service projects together. Working together for the Lord and for His people binds hearts together.

Express love and appreciation often for and to each other. In good marriages the spouses never tear the other down or belittle either the person or his or her accomplishments. They always strive to build each other up, to affirm positive traits, to let the other see his or her value in the other's eyes.

Chapter 23

COMMITTED FOR LIFE

Edna and Jack's/Julia and Al's Story

We were riding in a car with a young man, a relative of Peggy's. He'd met us at the airport, driven us many miles to visit with other relatives, and was now driving us back to meet another appointment. Charming and friendly, he had given up a day to accommodate us. He'd been most helpful and gracious. Though we had never met him before, we instinctively liked him.

As we rode along, he told us about his girlfriend, describing her in glowing terms. We asked if a wedding would take place soon. "I'm not sure," he replied. "You see, we're already living together—have been for more than a year."

"Well, if she's so wonderful, and you get along so nicely, why don't you just get married?" was our logical question.

He shook his head. "I just don't think I am ready for marriage."

We've no desire to judge this young man who isn't a Christian and presumably doesn't have the moral guidelines that many of us have been privileged to have. But we are left wondering why people who care about each other enough to cohabit consider themselves not ready to enter the covenant of marriage. Obviously they're afraid of commitment. Cohabitation leaves open a door by which they can back out if things turn out badly. They hold somewhere in the back of their minds that this might not work out, and it will be easier to break it off if they haven't actually been legally married.

They have a point. Marriage is a most solemn covenant that should never be entered into lightly. When He joined Adam and Eve together, God said: "Therefore a man leaves his father and his mother and clings to his wife, and they become one flesh" (Genesis 2:24, NRSV). Commenting on this verse, Walter Trobisch has written, "Cleaving [clinging] means love, but love of a special kind. It is a love which has made a decision and which is no longer a groping and seeking love. Love which cleaves is mature love, love which has decided to remain faithful—faithful to one person—and to share with this one person one's whole life" (*I Married You*, p. 16).

Jesus also commented on this verse: "So they are no longer two, but one flesh. Therefore what God has joined together, let no one separate (Matthew 19:6, NRSV).

Recall that day the bride and groom stood before the minister and the assembled witnesses and heard the charge: "And now, solemnly promising before God, and in the presence of these witnesses, will you, John, have this woman, Mary, to be your wedded wife, to live together after God's ordinance in the sacred estate of matrimony? Will you love her, comfort her, honor her, cherish her, in sickness and in health, in prosperity or adversity; and, forsaking all others, keep yourself only unto her as long as you both shall live? Do you so declare?"

Each partner answered, "I do!"

Talk about a serious promise! When you've taken a vow that awesome, how could you possibly renege on it? When "worse" happens in the "for better or for worse" pledge, does that release either one from so sacred a pledge? No wonder we are counseled not to enter into a marriage unless we mean to stay with it, come what may. "Leaving father and mother" means burning all our bridges behind us, with no way to go except forward. Ellen White gave some very direct counsel on this point:

"Every marriage engagement should be carefully considered, for marriage is a step taken for life. Both the man and the woman should carefully consider whether they can cleave to each other through the vicissitudes of life as long as they both shall live" (*The Adventist Home,* p. 340). "This vow links the destinies of the two individuals with bonds which naught but the hand of death should sever" *(ibid.).*

We certainly aren't intending to heap guilt on those who have gone through a divorce. People may be divorced through no fault of their own, and sometimes divorce is justified. We're talking to married couples who may be having difficulties in their relationship, encouraging them not to give up.

One of the things that hold a marriage together through thick and thin is that sense of commitment. There is hope for the couple who will say, "We're having serious trouble getting along. Sometimes we feel like killing each other. But we're committed to this marriage, and we're going to stick it out and make it work no matter what." Not that living in conflict is the ideal for marriage. But a solid commitment provides the motivation to work on the skills that will make the marriage truly happy and satisfying.

This can be illustrated by looking at the stories of two couples. One pair spent a career in high positions in denominational work with all the accompanying stresses. The other couple, after a working life in government, now devote their senior years to working for God. Both couples treasure their marriages in retirement.

Jack and Edna Harris have spent a lifetime together. Jack served as a pastor, union conference departmental director, president of the Oregon Conference, and secretary of the North Pacific Union Conference. He now serves as president of the Adventist Retirees Association. The pressures of a busy administrative career put a strain on any marriage. But because of their commitment to each other, they've worked through the problems and enjoy a happy married retirement. Jack tells their story.

We were like countless other young couples during World War II. We met at Plainview Academy. After graduation, military service called. We got married on a furlough, settled down after military discharge, went to college, got a call to the work, and our marriage has lasted more than 55 years and is still going. Now for some of the specifics.

We were freshmen at Plainview Academy in South Dakota. She was from a farm home; I was from a country home in the Black Hills. She was from a small Adventist family; I was one of 14 children in a non-Adventist home.

My parents lived so far back in the hills there was no possibility of high school for me without leaving home. I had attended a tiny country church school, operated by the only Adventists I had ever met or known. They invited me to attend their little school at no cost, and since their school was only a two-mile walk from my home (and the public school was a five-mile walk—uphill both ways in harsh, cold winter weather), I opted for the church school. In that way I became familiar with the Adventist Church to the extent that I was planning eventually to become a member. But I hadn't taken my stand yet.

When we graduated from the elementary school, my fellow classmate and I decided we would go to Plainview Academy, if it could be worked out. Well, it was worked out, all right. I worked every dime of my way through academy by milking cows, firing the school furnace, and anything else to pay off my bill. And I would do it again in a heartbeat.

On the third weekend after school started, I saw Edna in class one day and thought she was cute. I was too bashful to ask her for a date, so I wrote her a note asking her to be my date for the next Saturday night. I'm still waiting for her answer. For the rest of our academy years she went her way, and I went mine, seeing each other for four years but never having a date.

On the last Sunday of the school year, at the senior class picnic, I saw that she had no one special to eat with, and neither did I, so I invited her to join me. She jumped at the chance (my version of the story). We've been eating together steadily ever since.

Immediately after graduation I was inducted into the Army. I wrote to her every day and eventually proposed by mail. My proposal was accepted by mail. We agreed that when—and if—I came back from overseas, we would get married on the first furlough. When I did come back, though, Edna had started teaching church school just two weeks before I landed. In those days the conference wouldn't let teachers get married during the school year because it would set a wrong example to the elementary students (or some other equally rational reason). So I was home for 45 days, seeing her daily, but we couldn't get married. Right then we agreed that when I got my next furlough, we'd get married, with or without conference approval. So I came home for Christmas, and we got married—without asking permission. We just did it!

I received a call to serve as an intern in the Oklahoma Conference, where our second child, a son, was born, and where we served for six years. That was followed by a missionary stint to Brazil, which was a very rewarding experience for us.

We returned to the States, and the next years were filled with pastoral responsibilities, followed by departmental and administrative leadership on local conference and union conference levels, which took us through nearly 40 years of service across the nation.

Like countless other professional couples, we had our ups and downs in our married life. The fact that we both worked to put our children through college created its own stresses. There was so little time to be alone together. There was always some demand on her schedule or mine. The hardest were the administrative years, when I was president of the Oregon Conference. We went through the Desmond Ford debacle, the Harris Pine Mill closure mess, and the Davenport crisis, plus the closing of a beloved academy, with all that high emotion and furor. My phone rang off the hook night and day. Fortunately, in those days we had no cell phones, so people couldn't contact me when I was on the road, but they made up for it at the office and at home. There was never any peace or quiet for either of us. So tensions were high at times because closeness and quality togetherness were very limited in time and opportunity.

Looking back, it would seem I should have simply hung up the phone and ignored all those people. In reality, that doesn't work. So balancing domestic duties and privileges against professional responsibilities was often difficult, if not impossible. Edna had a very responsible job, and our schedules often didn't even whisper to each other, let alone wink at each other and say, "Let's do it."

But through it all, we stuck with it, had a great time, and would do it all again, because we knew that there were no other choices. Divorce was not an option or even a word in our vocabulary. We had our health, our home, our children, our ministry, and countless friends, and we both knew these problems would one day go away. Praise the Lord, they did, and we are still standing and loving more now than ever. It was worth it all, and a whole lot more. We would do it all over again in a heartbeat.

❖　❖　❖

Al and Julia McDowell had a career in military and civil service. In their retirement they are making a new vocation of serving the Lord. They reveal the same value of commitment as they both share their story.

❖　❖　❖

We both grew up during the Great Depression. This basically gave our marriage a sound financial foundation for it taught us to be thrifty. Al was employed by the federal government for 32 years. This employment included the Pearl Harbor attack on December 7, 1941. The first six years were in the Navy; the next 26 years were in civil service. Because Al could provide sound financial support, my career was full-time homemaker. We are the parents of one girl, Judy, who is an elementary school teacher.

Looking back over the years, we can see that the Lord has had His hand over our lives. When we were first married, Al was not an Adventist, even though I was. A death in my family had interrupted my education at Walla Walla College. After heavy military involvement during World War II, Al dedicated his life to serving God in any way that He would lead. This dedication finally led him to study and accept the Adventist message. This course of events has been a very growing experience for both of us.

The Lord has led us in many paths of duty for Him. We're presently heavily involved with Adventist World Radio. We've been privileged to travel to many churches and meetings to promote this wonderful work. We were honored to host the Adventist World Radio reception lounge during the General Conference session in Toronto. Our hearts are filled with a deep longing to see Jesus come. This provides a brief background of our lives together.

Probably, there isn't such a thing as a perfect marriage, but ours might come close. In reviewing our life together, we can recall no conflicts so serious that they required the services of a marriage counselor. From the very beginning we've been solidly committed to making this marriage work. We've always enjoyed doing things together. Our basic interest in life was building and nurturing a happy Christian home. During our 59 years together we've built nine homes and remodeled three others. We've been manually involved in the construction of these homes. We've lived in all of them. A marriage that can survive all these projects has to be pretty solid, but we've enjoyed every minute of it.

Having a purpose in our marriage and fulfilling that purpose has developed a strong stability in our relationship. We realized that without the support of each other, none of our projects would reach completion. We each brought our respective input. For example, Al was always interested in vacation time. He liked to plan exciting vacations to exotic places. I, on the other hand, grew up in a home where finances were very tight. Hard work was the story of my life, with no time for frivolous things such as vacations. The idea of taking time out and doing nothing but fun was hard for me at first, but I went along and am now game for almost anything. We've had some fabulous trips, including one to Australia and New Zealand, and still enjoy traveling together in our retirement.

We looked forward to a larger family, but the Lord didn't see fit to answer that particular prayer the way we had hoped. But we've learned to be happy with His plan and our one beautiful daughter. We're both avid vegetable gardeners. When spring comes, we can hardly wait to get the cultivator in the ground. This has been a very rewarding experience. It's also helped financially. We both have a burden to do something for the Lord. This has taken us into interesting avenues of service, such as our present work as volunteer representatives for Adventist World Radio.

One dark spot in our marriage has been the reaction of Al's family to his membership in the Adventist Church. I have been under terrific pressure all these years with Al's relatives constantly running down the Adventist Church. This problem has never been resolved and actually has become worse through the years. But this hasn't affected our relationship together. At this time we're very thankful to God for His love and guidance and for allowing us to keep busy working for Him. We're committed both to shaping our lives according to His will and to our very special marriage relationship. We guess you could say that this has been the secret of our marriage happily surviving for 59 years.

◆ ◆ ◆

These two stories illustrate the crucial importance of commitment and determination in helping a marriage survive the rough spots. And not just survive but flourish and grow.

Roger recently completed a 10-year longitudinal study of why teenagers drop out of or stay in the church (see *Why Our Teenagers Leave the Church* [Review and Herald, 2000]). The idea was to find out what factors in the lives of Adventist teenagers might predict who is still in the church in their mid-20s. Scores of items were examined, and many were predictive. However, the strongest factor was a response to this question: When you are grown and out on your own, do you still intend to be a member of the Adventist Church? Those who were "likely" or "highly likely" actually tended to still be with the church after 10 years than those who were "unlikely" or "not sure."

This is the psychological principle of commitment. People tend to stick with what they have determined to do. This is especially true when the commitment is announced publicly. It works for teenagers. It also works for married folks.

Stephen Chavez wrote in the *Adventist Review* (Feb. 8, 2001): "Marriage is not a life sentence for which you get 'time off for good behavior.' Marriage is a lifetime commitment with someone who shares your affections, values, and life goals. Having a successful marriage is not changing your partner, but reflecting God's unconditional love to him or her as often as you can, in as many ways as you can."

FINAL THOUGHTS

*I*n the dark days of World War II British Prime Minister Winston Churchill was invited to speak to a student body. When introduced, Churchill arose and made perhaps the shortest speech in political history. "Never give in, never give in, never, never, never, never." Seldom have so few words carried a nation through a time of crisis.

That has also been the message of this book. Hard times will come. Conflict will intrude. Love will seem to wane or disappear. That is not the time to lose courage. That is not the season to despair. That is not the moment to give up. The stories in this book have demonstrated that there is light at the end of the tunnel. There is life beyond discord. No matter what difficulties may cloud our relationships, we can work through them to a satisfying and hopeful future.

Artist and writer Lynda Barry, in a special edition of *Newsweek*, tells of growing up in a dysfunctional family. Her parents fought and finally separated. They were so immersed in their own problems that they had little time for her, and all the other families that she knew were in about the same shape.

Then she met a neighbor who was different. Mrs. Taylor actually listened to kids and took them seriously. She filled such an empty void in the child's life that Lynda hung around her house almost to the point of making a nuisance of herself. One morning she even slipped out and went next door while the Taylors were just getting up and making breakfast. She asked to eat with them, and here is what happened.

"I'll never forget that morning, sitting at their table eating eggs and toast, watching them talk to each other and smile. How Mr. Taylor made a joke and Mrs. Taylor laughed. How she put her hand on his shoulder as she poured coffee, and how he leaned his face down to kiss it. And that was all I needed to see. I needed to see it only once to be able to believe for the rest of my life that happiness between two people can exist."

That's it! The experiences of our couples testify that we can work through problems and find a joyful oneness. Happiness between two people really is possible. Never give up!

We have examined experiences that dealt with many types of concerns that could split a marriage and has often done so. Wrong priorities, hurt feelings, dividing time between job and family, financial difficulties, differences in temperament and personality, ups and downs, contrasting sexual needs and desires, blended families, instant motherhood, health crises, past abuse, male-female diversities, in-laws, children, conflicting ideas, and more.

We have explored methods by which successful couples have handled these concerns. Things such as putting God at the center of the marriage, taking their marital commitments very seriously, learning how to communicate feelings without blaming, developing conflict resolution skills, praying together every day, observing good models, discovering and meeting mutual needs, practicing "no-lose" decision-making skills, and putting the past behind them.

Have we covered every possible problem that could divide a couple? Certainly not! We would have liked to have included a story from a couple who was divided over child discipline (the softie and the strict one) and learned to work it out. This is one of the major issues over which married couples argue. Unfortunately, we couldn't find a couple willing to share their experience on this one. But the same skills of communication, conflict resolution, and decision-making that worked so well on other differences can also bridge this one. Parents need to understand that their primary relationship is with one another, so they must not let the children divide them. Some time in the future the children will grow up and move out, but husband and wife still have a life together. How they relate to each other while the children are still at home will predict how good that empty-nest life will be.

Another area that would be worth investigating is when one of the partners is unfaithful to the marriage vow. Obviously, this is a very sensitive subject, and frankly, we didn't have the courage to approach any couple to write about it. The Bible and the church have taken such infidelity to give permission to divorce and remarry. But because this is permitted doesn't mean it is mandated. Some mates have found a way to forgive; some couples have been able to put their lives back together and build a viable marriage. This requires all the skills covered in this book—putting God at the center, meeting each other's needs, making marriage a priority, deep and honest communication, conflict-resolution skills, and more.

We recognize that every case must be considered individually, and we don't want to suggest that divorce should never be an option. Still, a marriage is such a precious thing that it may be worth trying to save it. While we can't offer a couple with such a story, consider this short vignette by Judith Viorst ("Great Moments in Marriage," *Reader's Digest,* August 1982, pp. 7-10).

"Tom had left his wife and children for another woman, but Linda, his wife, refused him a divorce. She said that she still loved him and that he could still love her.

"One morning, after a night of empty sex and not much sleep, he drove to their house and saw his wife through the window getting the breakfast ready and the children off to school—as he said, 'doing what she had to do to keep their life, her life, *my* life, intact.'

"He was overcome with a sense of her commitment to holding together a warm, good life. He asked her that day to let him come back, recognizing that she was his very right, and much beloved, wife."

Perhaps one of the most powerful messages against divorce—of remembering the good and forgiving the bad—is found in song of a generation ago by Mexican-American singer Vikki Carr. In the song a woman is struggling over whether or not to sign the papers for the divorce her husband wants. Before she signs, she asks him to consider whether or not their lives will truly be better apart. She remembers the love that they shared. She asks whether he can really take care of their daughter alone and provide those things a little girl needs. Will he not have pangs of desire when he sleeps alone in the bed made for two? Can't all the good memories outweigh the problems they have had? If he doesn't agree, then she has no choice but to sorrowfully sign.

The song doesn't tell us how her husband responded; it leaves the question for us to answer. It is up to us—and you—to write the ending. That requires some serious thinking before taking the drastic divorce plunge.

So how shall we sum up this book? When we hold marriage seminars, we give those attending four prescriptions. We claim that if the couple will faithfully follow these prescriptions they will surely have a happy and wonderful marriage. Here they are:

1. *Pray with and for each other every day, preferably morning and evening.* When God is put at the center of a relationship, His blessing will make it succeed. Praying about each other's needs and praying together over common concerns is a binding force.

2. *Communicate with each other on a deep level.* By deep level we mean sharing not only ideas and solutions but feelings and emotions—our dreams, joys, goals, fears, disappointments, and even our anger and despair. It means that one will listen to the other carefully, without judgment, and try to restate those feelings and concerns so that the sending party knows that he or she has been understood.

3. *Spend both quantity and quality time together.* Make your relationship a priority. Play together, work together, do fun things together. Make every day unforgettable and build a wonderful memory bank of positive experiences.

4. *Affirm each other frequently.* Several times every day tell your partner what you love and admire about him or her. Eradicate criticisms. As the old song goes: "Accentuate the positive, eliminate the negative, latch on to the affirmative, and don't mess with mister in-between." You'll thrive in an atmosphere of peace and harmony.

Next to God's presence, a happy marriage is the most wonderful experience on earth. Go for it!